D1314132

faith limps

trusting a good God in a broken world

Michael Kelley

LifeWay Press®
Nashville, Tennessee

Published by LifeWay Press®
© 2012 Michael Kelley

ISBN 978-1-4158-7223-9
Item 005471380

Dewey decimal classification: 248.86
Subject headings: DISAPPOINTMENT \ PAIN \ SPIRITUAL LIFE

To order additional copies of this resource, write to LifeWay Church Resources Customer Service; One LifeWay Plaza; Nashville, TN 37234-0113; fax (615) 251-5933; phone toll free (800) 458-2772; order online at *www.lifeway.com;* e-mail *orderentry@lifeway.com;* or visit the LifeWay Christian Store serving you.

Printed in the United States of America

Leadership and Adult Publishing
LifeWay Church Resources
One LifeWay Plaza
Nashville, TN 37234-0175

contents

the author

Michael Kelley is a husband, father, author, and communicator who lives in Nashville, Tennessee, with his wife, Jana, and three children: Joshua, Andi, and Christian. After growing up in Texas, Michael moved to Birmingham, Alabama, and earned a master of divinity from Beeson Divinity School. Michael has served as a college and student pastor in churches in Tennessee and Texas, and he has preached at churches, conferences, and events across the country.

This Bible study is based on Michael's book *Wednesdays Were Pretty Normal*, the story of his family's journey through childhood cancer. Michael is also the author of three other Bible studies: *The Tough Sayings of Jesus, The Tough Sayings of Jesus 2,* and *Holy Vocabulary: Rescuing the Language of Faith.*

For more on Michael Kelley, find him online at *michaelkelleyministries.com,* where he is a daily blogger.

preface

On October 18, 2006, my family's life was altered forever. For us, it's "a date which will live in infamy"[1]—our personal Pearl Harbor or 9/11. Just as those days symbolize, for many Americans, times when the illusion of safety and security was shattered, October 18 was such a day for us.

My wife and I have a little boy named Joshua. He'd never had significant health problems, but on that day I found myself sitting in a pediatrician's office as he gave a preliminary diagnosis of leukemia—cancer of the blood.

In moments like this, everything we think we're so sure of about God, faith, and life suddenly becomes hazy. When we experience a job loss, a financial meltdown, the end of a relationship, or the death of a dream, we're forced to ask big questions about what it means to trust a good God in a broken world.

For a Christian, the result of such questions isn't so much an answer as God Himself. That's what this study is about: facing and embracing your pain and disappointment, then believing a good God will meet you in your difficult circumstances.

When we choose to face our pain, we will be changed. Our walk with God will be different. We will be forever marked, not only by our suffering but also by the One who loves us through it. Oh, we still walk with God on the other side of pain, but that walk is different. It's more like a limp.

My prayer through this study is that you will come to see that limping with Jesus isn't such a bad way to travel through life after all.

1. Franklin D. Roosevelt, presidential address to Congress, December 8, 1941.

between

Week 1
Group Experience

Getting Started

1. Introduce yourself and share one personal fact that will help your group know one another better.

2. Share what you hope to gain from this study.

3. Share with your group three experiences in your life, either positive or negative, that have shaped the person you are today.

Watch DVD session 1

Everyone has
a diagnosis day.

Walking On

1. Do you believe everyone has a diagnosis day? What does that mean to you?

2. When was your own personal diagnosis day?

3. How would you describe your relationship with God before that day? What about immediately after?

4. What kinds of questions about God and faith did you ask as a result of that experience?

5. What long-term effects do you think that experience has had on you?

6. What might be the value in reviewing that experience now?

Read week 1 and complete the activities before the next group experience.

Video sessions available for purchase at *www.lifeway.com/faithlimps*

between

It's not difficult to recognize when someone has something they need to tell you but don't really want to; you can almost sense the news coming. It's the same feeling you have when a news broadcaster interrupts the regularly scheduled programming for a special message. Or when your spouse talks on the telephone to someone in grave, hushed tones, only to hang up and invite you to have a seat because he or she has something to tell you. Or when your aging parents beat around the bush and make idle chitchat in their weekly call before saying, "There's something important we need to talk about."

That's the feeling I got one morning in October 2006 as my 2-year-old son played with his cars and trucks on the floor of the examination room in his pediatrician's office. He had what we thought was a harmless rash on his belly, but the doctor's tones implied something worse. He said the word that would come to be a regular part of our vocabulary from that day forward, and it felt as if a thousand-pound weight had been dropped onto my back: "Leukemia."

Two hours later the diagnosis was confirmed at Vanderbilt Children's Hospital. And our family was suddenly thrust into the experience that unites all humanity. Pain. Hardship. Difficulty. Disappointment. For Christians, these experiences remind us that we exist with one foot planted in heaven, where our true citizenship lies, and one foot planted on earth, where we are barraged by the realities of cancer, car accidents, job loss, infertility, and countless other troubles.

What does this mean for faith? For courage? For perseverance? What does this mean—to live between two worlds? It's a question that cancer forced us to answer. But we're not alone. If pain is the common denominator of humanity, then you've asked questions like that too.

Day 1
Life Is Pain

Do you remember where you were when you got the phone call? When you heard the news? When you received the diagnosis? Maybe it's etched in your mind, forever lodged and marked there as a pivotal moment when your life changed. Everyone has moments like this in life. They become markers, of a sort, and we use them to measure time.

There is the time before that event occurred, and there is the time after. And there are profound differences between those two times.

> **Has there been a specific turning point like that for you? Describe the circumstances.**

In what specific ways was your life different after that moment?

In what ways was your faith affected by that event?

All sorts of reactions might happen after that moment. Psychologists tell us there are five stages in the grief process: denial, anger, bargaining, depression, and eventual acceptance. But my suspicion is that it's not that clean and easy for most people. I believe for most of us, because these events are such pivotal markers, we don't simply accept them in the end. Rather, we stall out in them and then spend the rest of our lives just trying to get by. However, the incident is never too far from our minds.

Part of the reason we stall is because it's much easier to try and live with the new reality than it is to process it. It's too difficult to think deeply about it. To engage emotionally. To relive the moment, trying to understand just how profoundly we have been marked by loss.

If we stall, we will never ask the hard questions about the experience, particularly the questions about faith.

- ☐ Where is God?
- ☐ How could He let this happen?
- ☐ Did He cause this to happen?
- ☐ Is this punishment for something I've done?
- ☐ Is God even real?

Have you ever asked questions similar to these?

What other specific questions related to your faith did you ask in the midst of difficult circumstances?

If we want to engage those questions, let's start at the very beginning. The truth is, you can trace every occurrence of pain, loss, and disappointment back to one source. Regardless of your circumstance, the initial cause of that circumstance was sin.

Reflect on the previous statement. Do you agree with it? Why or why not?

In what sense might sin be the cause of all pain and loss?

Perhaps you're familiar with the story in Genesis 3. A man. A woman. A perfect world and perfect fellowship with God. Then a snake. An apple. And a choice. That choice first sent shock waves of pain reverberating through the universe.

Read this story for yourself in Genesis 3:1-19. List the effects
of sin detailed in this passage.

Now read Romans 8:22-23. According to Paul, how far-reaching
are the effects of sin?

We typically think of sin as doing something bad. It's certainly that, but sin goes
far wider and deeper than mere actions. In humanity sin is not just an action but
a heart bent toward evil. It's the condition that makes us delight in doing wrong
instead of doing right. And beyond the scope of humanity, sin has also plunged
creation into decay. Tornadoes, earthquakes, and droughts are just as much an
effect of the fall in Genesis 3 as lying, lust, and murder.

If we begin to think of sin in these far-reaching terms, we will see that pain indeed
links all humanity together. Wherever we come from, whatever our occupations
are, and whatever course our lives take, we all exist in a sinful world. Because we
do, we've all experienced its dreadful effects.

Pain indeed links all humanity together.

How do you typically think of sin? Check all that ap

☐ Sin is the bad things I do.
☐ Sin is the universal human condition—a he
  that continually wants to do evil.
☐ Sin explains why we have natural disasters:
  all creation is in a fallen state.

Why did you answer that way?

Why might it be important to consider the universal reach of
sin as you wrestle with the meaning of your own pain and loss?

Consider today that everywhere you go, everyone you come in contact with
lives in the same world you do—a world of sin and pain. Take a moment and
reflect on the people you come in contact with, remembering that they too
have experienced the effects of the fall.

Day 2
A Foot in Each World

Perhaps the best place on earth to see the commonality of human pain is in the emergency room. Walk in there, and it suddenly ceases to matter whether you're rich or poor, black or white, clean or dirty. The ER is one of those places where the stark but often unspoken reality of the desperate human condition comes to the surface. There you find people who are aware they are united. They are united in pain. In desperation. In hardship.

We got to know emergency rooms very well during the early days of Joshua's treatment for leukemia. When a person undergoes chemotherapy and gets a fever, the only response is to go to the hospital. Fevers can be very dangerous during times of treatment because chemotherapy attacks a person's immune system, making them susceptible to all sorts of infections. We spent many hours trying to entertain our son in ERs, all the while trying to keep him from taking off his hospital mask, which we hoped was keeping more germs from entering his little body.

During those times we found ourselves turning our eyes to heaven and praying as never before. There's nothing like desperation to focus your prayers. We prayed for healing, for relief, and for divine intervention in our situation. We prayed the way Paul prayed in 2 Corinthians 12.

Read 2 Corinthians 12:7b-10. What was Paul struggling with?

What did Paul ask the Lord to do?

What, in your own words, was the answer Paul received?

The word *skolops* in Greek can mean *thorn* (see v. 7b), but sometimes the word is translated *stake*. It has a violent connotation; *stake* doesn't conjure up warm and fuzzy images when referring to pain. Instead, I picture almost savage pain. This leads us to believe Paul wasn't talking about a habitual moral sin he continued to struggle with; it was real physical pain.

And not just a little pain either. This was a continual, throbbing sort of pain that accompanied the apostle wherever he went. Some believe his ailment was severe headaches, which would certainly explain Paul's eye trouble that he mentioned at the close of the Book of Galatians. Others say it was a recurring malaria fever that he picked up on one of his island adventures. Those who have suffered a similar disease compared their pain to the pain of a dentist's drill boring down.

> **Is it surprising to you that the Lord would not take the pain away? Why or why not?**

> **Read the strange passage that precedes these verses in 2 Corinthians 12:1-7a.**

Paul described a glorious vision of heaven. He was enraptured. He experienced the fullness of joy, the essence of existence. He was living in the indescribable greatness of eternity. But not for long.

Imagine being caught up to heaven like that and then crashing back to earth. Further imagine that what sends you back to earth is the thorn. The pain. The ache. The sadistic dentist ceaselessly drilling into your head. That's a rude awakening, but maybe a fall like that feels familiar to you. It's the feeling of having a good, right, and blessed life—and then suddenly being brought back to earth by your thorn.

> **Can you identify with Paul in this crash? What specific moment comes to mind?**

Maybe you are suffering with a thorn now. If so, what is it?

Have you asked God to remove your thorn? What answer did you receive?

As Christians we can identify with Paul because we truly have a foot in each of two worlds. Once we accept Christ, we have a new home, and it's not here. The Bible reminds us that we will experience trouble of all kinds here on earth. Jesus said, "You will have suffering in this world. Be courageous! I have conquered the world" (John 16:33). Because we're in Christ, our ultimate treasure and citizenship are in heaven. So we're citizens of heaven, but we're living here. We have one foot planted in heaven and one foot planted on earth. We live between joy and pain. Between glory and dejection. Between elation and depression.

We live between joy and pain. Between glory and dejection. Between elation and depression.

Look back at 2 Corinthians 12:9-10. Instead of removing the thorn, what did God grant Paul?

Is that comforting for you? Why or why not?

Most of the time our thorns aren't removed. We still have to take the pills. We still have to go to the treatments. We still have to wake up and haul ourselves out of bed in the morning. But amazingly, God promises that the days when we are at the end of our rope are also the days when His sustaining grace and strength will be most visible and apparent. He doesn't promise to remove the pain, but He promises that in the midst of it, His grace will sustain us.

How have you specifically sensed God's grace sustaining you in hard times?

How have you seen His grace when dealing with your thorn?

Believing in that grace for today must be a choice. And tomorrow? It will be a choice then too. But perhaps it's helpful to recognize that we aren't the only ones who know what it's like to be caught between heaven and earth. For this sustaining grace comes from One who was raised up on two crossbeams, physically positioned not quite in the air and yet not quite on earth. It comes from One who knows what life is like between two worlds, who gave up so much to suffer on this earth for our sakes. So when we look into the face of Jesus, we can know that when we are weak, we are strong.

Pray today for the strength to believe in God's sustaining grace. Acknowledge that the thorn might not go away, but express your firm trust that He will sustain you for another day.

Day 3
Desperate Faith

We recognize that sin has dramatically affected all humanity. We acknowledge that as Christians we can trust in the sustaining grace of God. But we would be naive to think life-altering experiences that involve pain and suffering would leave our faith unscathed.

When you engage your painful circumstances, you may witness a collision between what is happening and what you hope is true. You don't want to doubt, much less renounce, the timeless truths you believe: that God is good, He is powerful, He chooses at times to heal and at times not to, and He is always right and loving in His choices. But those assumptions are tested during pain. It's where the prover-bial rubber meets the road as your belief system has a head-on collision with reality.

Define *faith*.

Is faith more than just an intellectual agreement to facts about God? Why or why not?

During your times of pain, have you asked God the difficult questions? Which ones?

Did you get any answers? What were they?

What is faith? What does it mean to believe? If we want to rely on faith during trials, surely we must examine what we're trying to hang on to. Up to the collision, most of us implicitly define *faith* more in terms of what it's not rather than what it is. In those terms *faith* is defined as *not doubting*. It's the absence of questions. It's obediently following God without hesitation.

> Read Hebrews 11:1. Is that what this verse means—
> not doubting, not questioning? Why or why not?

You see the obvious problem. That definition of *faith* works as long as everyone is healthy, there's plenty of money in the bank, and the cars are working fine. But if faith is the absence of doubt, where does that leave you when all you have is doubt? If faith is not asking questions, what do you do when all you have is questions? If faith is absolute certainty, how do you respond when nothing in your life feels certain anymore?

With questions like that, we might turn to Scripture to find a prescription for times of life like these. Maybe a clarification of faith. Perhaps an expanded definition. But instead, there's a passage of Scripture that might be encouraging. It's not so much a definition as a story. It became very meaningful to me as I sat in dark hospital rooms, listening to the labored breathing of a hurting little boy in the bed next to me. For in this story I found a father who, like me, was powerless to help his own son.

> Read Mark 9:14-25. What one word would you use to describe
> the father in this passage?

Let's not stop at reading the text. Think deeper and read between the lines to learn this man's backstory.

> What led that father to the base of the mountain on that day
> so long ago?

List the elements of the disease the father described.

The father claimed his son had been in this state since childhood, which indicates that maybe he wasn't a child anymore. Perhaps his son had passed the age of 13, the traditional coming-of-age moment in Jewish culture. If so, the son was now an adolescent, meaning this affliction had followed them for years.

Maybe as the father revealed the nature of his boy's condition, pictures flooded his mind. All the times they were having dinner with friends when their son tipped the food bowls over with his shaking. The days when everything was normal until he looked out of the house to see his son lying once again in the dirt. The times he'd held his son's head close to his chest as he cried because the other little boys were making fun of him.

They lived in a culture that looked at disease and misfortune as a curse from the Lord. So perhaps the father's business suffered. Maybe he struggled to find work because no one wanted to do business with the community pariah. And maybe even his relationship with his wife had deteriorated. Surely there was no time for intimacy when they had to keep watch on their son.

Given the previous description, would you change the one word you used to describe the father?

Can you sympathize with the father's desperation? In what way?

Much like Paul, here was a man with a thorn of sorts. And here he was, asking Jesus to remove it. But how would Jesus respond?

Think about your own backstory. Can you isolate some ways your experience of pain has affected the rest of your life? Are they positive or negative?

Day 4
"If ..."

If we look deep inside the words of this hurting father (see Mark 9:14-25), we might just find a reflection of ourselves. When we're in pain, we do the same thing this man did: we come to Jesus. We do the same thing Paul did: we ask Jesus to take it away. That's what I did for Joshua anyway.

But here's the question: Do we really believe God is going to do anything about it? Or have we prayed one too many times without feeling we got anything in return? Perhaps that's why my own prayers were always somewhat guarded. I wanted to believe God could and would heal my son. But I couldn't help the overwhelming sense of dread and doubt that tainted my requests.

> Do you really believe God listens and acts in response to your prayers about your pain? Why or why not?

> Does the way you pray reflect how strongly you believe this? How?

Perhaps the father in Mark 9 felt something similar. Did he really believe Jesus would do something, or did he come that day with low expectations? Surely this was not the first "healer" he had approached to help his son. He had been disappointed before. Maybe all he had was the fleeting thought that this time would be different. But it looked as though he would be disappointed in this rabbi as well. After all, when he got there, Jesus wasn't even around. And when He finally showed up, He hardly seemed compassionate about the situation.

> Go back and read Jesus' reaction to the man's story in Mark 9:19. What emotion do you sense in Jesus?

Why might Jesus have responded the way He did?

Is this how you would expect Jesus to respond to a desperate situation like this? Why or why not?

Jesus walked into an incredibly frustrating situation. His disciples were there, and because of their pride, they lacked the humility and faith to help the boy. The Pharisees were there too, and they certainly didn't believe in Jesus. And then there was the father, who couldn't possibly begin to grasp whom he was talking to. No one present that day could muster enough faith to believe.

But at least the father was honest: "If You can do anything, have compassion on us and help us" (v. 22).

If. If You are able. If You are loving enough. If you are powerful enough. If You are who people say You are. The *if* betrayed the father's doubt. But despite the *if,* he pleaded with Jesus. Literally he said, "Be moved in your bowels." Not a pleasant thought to us, but for the Jewish people at that time, the bowels were considered the deepest part of a person, the emotional center of a person's being: "Be moved in Your guts, in the deepest parts of who You are, and help us."

Have you ever pleaded with Jesus like that? When?

Have you ever prayed with an *if* like that? When? How did God respond?

After his request Jesus turned the tables on the father. This is where the story gets really uncomfortable. I distinctly remember reading and identifying with this man late one night in the hospital. Joshua had finally fallen to sleep, lulled by repetitive watching of a Barney video. And I felt very alone and very frightened. Jesus' response did little to ease my fears.

"If You can?" said Jesus. "Everything is possible to the one who believes" (v. 23). "The question is not whether I can. *I can.* Believe Me, I can. No, the question is actually more about you than about Me. It's not about My ability; it's about your faith. Do you really believe I can?"

That's difficult to stomach because in those desperate times we know our faith is hanging on by a thread. The thought that healing or deliverance or relief depends on us is devastating because we know in our deepest parts we really don't believe. Not fully. Not wholly.

And neither did this father. But then we see how we are typically different from him. Our tendency when our faith is less than perfect is to hide it. To act as if we believe. To simply push doubt out of our mind. But not this man. Rather than trying to find the perfect prayer, he said exactly what he felt. Exactly what he knew. Exactly what he believed or, in his case, what he didn't believe.

> How honest would you say you are with God about your faith in His ability to help your situation?

> In what types of situations are you prone to be less honest with God?

In your prayer time today try to have a completely honest conversation with God. Remind yourself that you're not telling Him anything He doesn't already know. Confess the deepest doubts and fears of your heart.

Day 5
Filling Up What We Lack

"I do believe! Help my unbelief" (Mark 9:24). Some ancient texts of this passage say the father exclaimed this through his tears. In an emotional outburst the man actually owned up to his doubt. How pathetic. How undignified. How unspiritual. How … honest.

And then the impossible happened. Jesus healed the boy—just like that. After years of struggle, gallons of tears, and immeasurable heartbreak and frustration, it was finished. The miraculous happened, but in the wake of that tremendous event, we might legitimately ask, "Why?"

What was the qualification Jesus gave to the father in order to see this healing?

Did the father meet Jesus' terms? Why or why not?

This is a pivotal issue for those who know what it's like to see their faith hanging on by a thread. It's so pivotal because when we're in the hospital, or staring at unpaid bills, or waiting by the window for a child to come home, or enduring another seemingly hopeless situation, we want to believe. We try to believe. But in our most honest moments, we know we don't completely believe. This man experienced the very same doubts we have. Yet Jesus acted on his behalf.

Maybe Jesus acted because He's Jesus. He was so overcome by the depth of this man's emotion that it was as if He said, "It's true that you don't have enough faith for Me to do this. But from My goodness and love I will make an exception."

Perhaps Jesus looked around at the crowd and decided the situation was getting out of control. It was time to put an end to this. So He healed the kid because it was the quickest, cleanest, and easiest way out of there.

But maybe Jesus saw in this man the very thing He didn't see in the teachers of the law and even in His own disciples. Maybe Jesus found exactly what He was looking for in the man's emotional outburst. Maybe in the father's confession of his faithlessness, Jesus found the faith He had been looking for all along.

How can that be? How might this man's confession of doubt actually contain faith?

Respond to this statement: "This father had the faith to doubt."

This father does not teach us how to have perfect faith. But he does teach us about the nature of faith in a broken world. Real faith is not necessarily the absence of doubts; real faith is about coming to Jesus with what you have. When you have doubts and come to Jesus anyway, you're expressing faith in Him rather than faith in your ability to have faith.

Real faith is about coming to
Jesus with what you have.

Do you understand that distinction? In your own words write the difference between having faith in Jesus and having faith in your ability to have faith.

When you come to Jesus even when you have doubts, you're expressing that you believe Jesus is bigger than your questions. Bigger than your unbelief. Bigger than your doubts.

When you think about it, this is really the core of Christianity. You come to Jesus as you are, with all your sin and brokenness, and trust Him to respond. God is faithful to do that, for the gospel is about God's making up for what we lack.

When we come to initial faith in Christ, we confess that we possess nothing that could possibly merit God's love and favor, and we declare that in the cross Jesus makes up for what we lack. That pattern is no different after we become Christians.

If you are struggling with a hardship or a thorn, what doubts are you dealing with?

Have you brought your doubts to God and asked Him to help with your unbelief? Why or why not?

How have you seen God making up for your lack of faith in this situation?

In our daily walk with Him, God is still making up for what we lack. It's amazing and glorious to think that even now, in the middle of our doubt and fear, Jesus Himself lives to intercede for us at the right hand of the Father (see Heb. 7:25). He's praying for us right now. And in moments when we don't know what or even how to pray, the Holy Spirit intercedes for us with deeper, more emotional, and more pure groanings and pleadings than we can possibly understand (see Rom. 8:26).

Given all that, what's left for us is to have the faith in God just to come to Him. To be honest with God—good, bad, and ugly included. We come to Jesus not as we aren't but as we are. And when we do that, we show that we believe Jesus can make up for all we lack.

Pray again today in a completely honest way. As you do, remind yourself that the Son and the Spirit are already aware of your suffering and are interceding with you. Pray as you are and not as you aren't, as you can and not as you can't.

tears

Week 2
Group Experience

Looking Back

1. Share one insight you gained from your study of week 1 in the workbook.

2. Did this week's study cause you to look at doubt any differently? What about faith?

3. How do you think God feels about the suffering of His children?

4. If God doesn't like the fact that we suffer, why doesn't He stop it?

5. Have you ever been completely honest with God about a hardship you were going through? If so, what did you say? How do you think God viewed your honesty? How did He respond?

Watch DVD session 2

Jesus wept.

Walking On

1. Have you ever felt that Jesus was absent? When?

2. During that time what were your emotions like?

3. Can you see any purpose behind Jesus' seeming inattentiveness?

4. How do you think Jesus felt about your situation during that time?

5. How does thinking about Jesus' emotional reaction to your suffering make a difference in your life?

Read week 2 and complete the activities before the next group experience.

Video sessions available for purchase at *www.lifeway.com/faithlimps*

tears

We live between heaven and earth, and because we do, there is no escape from pain and loss in life. These experiences mark us; they become the sign-posts of our time on earth. We pray, we seek, we long, and we trust God to intervene and make His presence come to bear on our circumstances.

As our son's treatment for cancer stretched from days into months, we began to accept that the road we were on was a long one. On the worst days Joshua was hooked to a constant morphine drip—something to alleviate or at least lessen his constant pain. But my wife and I had no emotional morphine drip. We didn't have anything to deaden the fear and doubt. Or the anger.

On the long road it often felt that our prayers hit the ceiling above us and bounce straight back down to earth. It was during those times that our prayers took on an air of frustration: "Where is God? What is He doing? Why isn't He springing into action? Doesn't He care?"

It was on that long road that we came to identify with two sisters in John 11 who discovered not just a God who can heal but also a God who can weep.

Day 1
Sick ... and Loved

What do you do with a waiting Jesus? We know how to react to the loving Jesus. We can understand the passionate Jesus. We can even deal with the angry Jesus. We certainly see all of these attributes of His personality displayed in the Gospels. But a waiting Jesus? That's a problem.

It's a problem because during times of extreme duress, waiting is about the furthest thing from what we think Jesus is supposed to do. He's supposed to care. To heal. To fix. But in John 11 He seemingly did none of that. At least not at first.

> Read John 11:1-6. What can you assume about Jesus' relationship with this family, based on these verses?

> Given that they were close friends, does Jesus' inaction surprise you? Why or why not?

> Have you ever felt Jesus was intentionally waiting to show up in the midst of your circumstances?

We should feel a certain kinship with the family mentioned in John 11. Mary, Martha, and Lazarus weren't just acquaintances with Jesus. They weren't faces in the crowd or casual bystanders to His ministry. Whenever Jesus traveled through the region of Bethany, He made time for this sister-sister-brother trio. He ate with them. He talked and laughed with them. These people were like His family.

It makes sense, then, that when one of them became gravely ill, they sent word to Jesus. Notice the intimate quality of their message. They didn't say, "Hey, Jesus, that guy You met one time on a hillside—remember him? He's sick." No, it was much more intimate than that: "Lord, the one You love is sick" (v. 3).

Don't we do the same thing? According to the Bible, we're the ones Jesus loves. He loves us at the cost of His own life. When we find ourselves in desperate situations, we send word to Jesus too, saying, "Someone You love needs You." In fact, we send word to Jesus because we're commanded to do so.

Read James 5:13-15. Which situation in this passage relates to you now?

Why do you think we are commanded to pray in all of these circumstances?

What does this command reveal about God's character?

Jesus gets our messages, just as He got the message from Mary and Martha. The problem comes with what He did with it or rather what He didn't do with it.

Look back at John 11:1-6. What did Jesus do when He heard Lazarus was sick?

Put yourself in the place of Mary and Martha. What must they have been thinking when they sent the message?

What about when the hours and days passed without a word from Jesus?

We can imagine what it must have been like for the sisters, because most of us have been in a similar situation. You fervently ask Jesus to heal. To provide a job. To bring home a wayward child. And yet nothing seems to happen.

You fervently ask Jesus to heal. To provide a job. To bring home a wayward child. And yet nothing seems to happen.

I imagine the sisters must have sat by their brother's bed, watching him sweat out a fever. Seeing him squirm and moan in his sleep, wondering whether they should summon the doctor again. Every once in a while getting up and walking to the window to see whether someone was coming up the walk. Expecting, hoping maybe this would be the day when Jesus would show up, because in their hearts they knew if only He would, everything would change. But then each day waking up and seeing that things were getting worse instead of better. Then going to sleep each night wondering, *Where is our miracle?*

This wasn't a stretch for me. My 2-year-old son began each morning by taking chemotherapy pills. At that time he was so young that the concept of swallowing something without chewing it was as foreign as learning quantum physics. So my wife and I became masters of crushing up various kinds of oral medications, carefully scraping them from the counter onto a spoon, then covering them with chocolate syrup. Then we would feed the concoction to our son, all the while wondering when Jesus was going to show up and end it all. Like the sisters, we believed Jesus loved us. And like the sisters, the days kept ticking away.

> Have you ever been in a situation when you called on Jesus, but He didn't show up? Maybe you're waiting now for Him to show up in your suffering. What does it feel like to wait on Jesus? What thoughts go through your head day after day?

How does this wait affect your faith? The way you pray? The way you live your life?

If we're the people Jesus loves, we can only conclude that there must be some reason for His waiting. But what?

As you pray today, express your emotions to Jesus. Recall times when you have waited and felt as if nothing were happening. Maybe you're waiting now as you face a difficult circumstance. Confess your confidence in the wisdom of God, but don't fail to be honest with Him about how it feels to wait.

Day 2
Waiting on Purpose

Let's leave the scene at Bethany for a few moments to contemplate another portion of Scripture in which we find a disturbing, uncomfortable account of a waiting Jesus. In Mark 4 we don't find Jesus waiting; we find Him sleeping, of all things. Now I suppose that wouldn't be so unusual except for the fact that His followers, those closest to Him in mission as well as in proximity, were caught in a desperate situation.

> Read Mark 4:35-41. Put yourself in the place of the disciples. What would you have been thinking as the storm blew in?

> Given the strength of the storm, why do you think Jesus was able to sleep so soundly?

Let's not sell the courage of the disciples too short here. At first glance we might deem them as cowards, considering the whining nature of their complaint against Jesus: "Don't you care that we're going to die?" (v. 38).

Really? You're going to die? It can't be that bad, can it? A little rain? Some wind too? But we mustn't forget whom we're dealing with here. These were experienced fishermen who had grown up, lived on, and survived by the sea. They were very familiar with all kinds of weather patterns, including storms. Surely this wasn't the first time they'd been caught in a storm on the water.

But this storm was evidently so intense that it softened the callous hearts of these grizzled fishermen. For them to claim they were going to die doesn't point to their fear as much as it points to the ferocious nature of the storm around them. With that we can surely identify.

> How would you describe your feelings during a particularly difficult season of your life? Did it feel like a storm? How?

If you think back to the most difficult time in your life and try to come up with a metaphor for it, it might even read much like this passage. Wind. Rain. Flashing lightning. Rolling, deep thunder. It was the feeling of being swept around and helpless because you were in the grip of something over which you had no control. You were beaten and tossed by the circumstances around you, so much so that it felt as if you literally couldn't get out of bed for one more day.

And yet Jesus was asleep in the boat.

> Is there any significance in the fact that Jesus was actually in the boat with the disciples during the storm? What is it?

> Look back at Jesus' reaction in verse 39. What do you imagine His voice sounded like?

Though He might have seemed absent due to slumber, Jesus was nevertheless present with His disciples. They were not alone, though they must have felt so. And when Jesus finally awakened, I don't sense a trace of panic in His voice. I imagine Him stretching as if He'd just been dozing in a hammock between two trees, rocked back and forth by a gentle breeze. Then with one word He changed everything. And "there was a great calm" (v. 39).

But it might be pertinent for us to ask the question of why Jesus was sleeping in the boat to begin with. The simple answer is that He was tired. But perhaps there's more there.

> **What might be another reason Jesus chose to take a nap at this time?**

> **What did the whole situation eventually lead to in the hearts of the disciples?**

We may say many things about Jesus. We may say He's troubling, frustrating, or confusing, but we can't say He's arbitrary. Even in His meandering way of teaching and preaching through the countryside, we sense a great intentionality, though it might not be apparent to those examining a map. Here too He didn't just happen to fall asleep. There was purpose in His sleeping.

> **Have you waited on God enough to discover any purposes He had for your waiting? What were they?**

This account brought the disciples a huge step closer to an understanding of just whom they were dealing with. The result was a great display of Jesus' power and the worship of the disciples. In a situation that felt radically out of control, there was divine intention behind it. Even in sleep.

In a situation that felt radically out of control, there was divine intention behind it.

Could the situation be any different for Mary and Martha? We can't believe Jesus simply took His time because He wanted to take the long way to Bethany, maybe to catch some tourist sights along the way. No. There must be a reason behind His waiting. And if that's the case for them, it must be the case for us too.

As you pray today, consider what those times felt like when you were waiting for Jesus. Express your faith in His intentionality, though you might not know what His intentions were. If you're waiting now, pray about your feelings in this situation.

Day 3
God Loves ... God

Embracing the truth of Jesus' intentionality helps us immensely when the storm is raging around us. Or when the brother in the bed keeps getting sicker. Although we may not understand what God is doing while He's waiting, we can doggedly cling to the truth that He is indeed doing *something*.

But perhaps if we search further, we might discover a more specific answer to the question of why Jesus is waiting to respond to our crisis.

> Read John 11:4-7. What did Jesus say would be the result of Lazarus's sickness?

> What is the glory of God, in your own words?

> How often do you think about and prioritize the glory of God?

Jesus said this whole experience was meant to glorify God. That's odd, because you would think the opposite would be the case. Wouldn't it have glorified God if Jesus had miraculously snapped His fingers or wiggled His nose and Lazarus had jumped to his feet dancing? I suppose it would.

But there's a strategy in Jesus' actions. It's one thing for someone to say, "I just got bumped up to a six-figure income, bought a house in the suburbs, and have a beautiful spouse and 2.5 healthy children. Glory to God!" Glory to God indeed. No doubt He's the giver of all good gifts (see Matt. 7:11). But it's a different matter when people are weeping over the state of their circumstances, their health, and their world, yet they are able to say along with Job, "I know that my Redeemer lives" (Job 19:25, NASB). There's a certain power in that scenario that is somehow lacking in the first one.

What makes the second scenario more powerful than the first?

Does anyone in your life spring to mind when you think of that kind of God-honoring attitude? Who is it?

What are the key practices that mark their lives, enabling them to express that kind of faith?

But there's a problem with Jesus' motivation here. Jesus was fully human but also fully divine. So when Jesus was pursuing the glory of God, He was actually pursuing His own glory. And this is just one of many passages in the Bible that display God's love for Himself.

Read the following passages. Record what each identifies as bringing glory to God.

Isaiah 43:6-7

Isaiah 43:25

John 14:13

Romans 9:17

Ephesians 1:4-6

1 Peter 2:12

Does it bother you that God seeks His own glory? Why or why not?

It's this very notion—that God is utmost and chief in His own affections—that bothered C. S. Lewis to no end and was one of the final walls to fall before his conversion to Christianity. To put it simply, how could we love a God who is so selfish? So arrogant? So egomaniacal?

After all, if God is the ultimate, true author of Scripture, then every time the psalms exhort us to worship Him, God is essentially saying to the world, "Praise Me! Praise Me! Praise Me!" To Lewis this sounded like a petulant child more than a God worthy of worship.

Is it wrong for God to seek our worship?

Is it wrong for a person to desire self-worship?

What is the difference between the two?

There's a huge difference between God's pursuit of His own glory and a person's pursuit of his or hers. When a person, no matter how good, does this, he's a liar at his core. For no person is ultimately good, beautiful, powerful, and holy enough to warrant praise. But God is.

In fact, for God to seek something other than His own glory would mean He loved something more than it deserves to be loved. When we do that, we say we have an idol in our lives. If God did that, He would compromise His perfection. He would be an idolater.

That means we're wrong to think God loves us more than anything else in the universe, enough to put our interests above His own. He does not. He loves Himself, and it's right and good for Him to do so, because He is worthy.

We're wrong to think God loves us more than anything else in the universe, enough to put our interests above His own.

Describe a time when God ultimately received glory through a hardship in your life.

But just because it's right and good for God to demand our worship—in good times and bad—doesn't mean there aren't also profound implications in doing so. Just ask Mary and Martha.

Express in prayer today the greatness of God. Reaffirm your desire to love and pursue His glory as much as He loves and pursues it. Reflect on ways God might be gaining glory through your painful circumstance.

Day 4
The Consequences X

Maybe you can identify ways God has been glorified through your circumstances. Perhaps others who are walking through similar situations have found great encouragement and strength in observing your response to trials. Or maybe your own pain has made you more compassionate as you empathize with others who are struggling.

> Read 2 Corinthians 1:3-4. According to this passage, what is one way God uses painful circumstances in the lives of His children?

> Have you seen that dynamic at play in your life or in the life of another person? Describe what happened.

There are also unintended ways God might use our pain for His glory. These are as numerous as the creative dimensions of God. Perhaps it's through a web of relationships in which you were able to testify to God's grace during your hardship. Maybe it's through a blog or journal you kept during times of difficulty. Or maybe it's through teaching a Sunday School class or leading a Bible study.

Whatever the case, if you're a child of God, you can be sure God will work your circumstances for His glory: "All things work together for the good of those who love God: those who are called according to His purpose" (Rom. 8:28). That's what would happen not only in the case of Lazarus but also in the case of my son Joshua. People would pay us kind compliments about the way they perceived we were handling this situation, describing in detail how our supposed strong faith had led them to greater depth in their relationship with Jesus. There was no doubt God was gaining glory through our situation.

But even though we might have accepted the purpose behind Jesus' waiting, we still had to deal with the consequences of the delay.

> Read John 11:17-32. What were some of the consequences of Jesus' waiting?
>
> Physical consequences:
>
> Mental consequences:
>
> Why might John have included the specific detail of how long Jesus waited before coming?
>
> Do you identify with either one of the sisters in this passage more closely? Which one? Why?

Lazarus died. The sisters mourned. The community was disheartened. In fact, to make sure we got the full impact of Jesus' decision, John included the specific detail of how long Jesus waited and then how long Lazarus had been in the grave. John 11:6 says Jesus stayed where He was for two more days. Then it took two additional days for Him to reach Bethany. The fact that "Lazarus had already been in the tomb four days" (v. 17) is a significant detail in this story because it left no doubt about his fate. In those days, when there were no heart monitors, it was not uncommon for people to be pronounced dead, only to wake up from a comatose state. In fact, after someone was assumed to be dead, people examined the body, even going to the cemetery to do so, up to three days after death, just to make sure.

When John wrote "four days," he meant to communicate there was no hope left in Bethany. Lazarus was gone. He was undeniably dead.

What impact does the certainty of Lazarus's death have on your understanding of the miracle that was coming?

By this time Mary and Martha had entered the traditional period of mourning for their brother. Jesus' inaction might result in the glory of God, but it had also resulted in tremendous grief for the sisters. We see that those sisters dealt with their grief in different ways.

Compare the reactions of Mary and Martha when they saw Jesus. How would you characterize each?

God's glory often comes at a tremendous price. It did for Mary and Martha. Perhaps it has for you. But we have the luxury of reading the end of this story. We know Lazarus will not be in the grave for long. But our own stories might not have such happy endings.

Our own stories might not
have such happy endings.

Maybe you're waiting for God to show up to relieve your suffering. What have been the consequences of waiting?

Physical effects:

Emotional effects:

Relational effects:

Spiritual effects:

Are you confident that your situation will bring glory to God? Why or why not?

What, then, are we to do when there is the promise of heaven but no promise of earthly relief or healing? What are we to make of a God who expects us to make sacrifices for His own glory? How are we supposed to regard a child with cancer who doesn't seem to be getting better but is nonetheless bringing glory to God?

Consider these difficult questions for the rest of the day. Spend time thinking and praying through them, applying them to your specific situation. Record your thoughts to read again later.

Day 5
Immanuel

We might understand and even accept that our painful circumstances will be used for the glory of God. Still, there are unresolved issues because of the casualties left in the wake: What about my daughter? What about my father? What about my career? What about my dreams?

> What are some casualties that may result from your current hardship, even though God may receive glory?

All of these priorities might fall to the wayside for the sake of God's glory. So how does God respond when presented with questions like these? We get the answer from the grieving sisters.

> Read another story of Mary and Martha in Luke 10:38-42. What does this passage reveal about the personalities of Mary and Martha? How were they different?

> Are you more like Mary or Martha? How?

> How might that personality handle issues of loss and grief differently?

John 11 seems to indicate that Martha was a little more ready to accept Lazarus's death than her sister. She met Jesus outside town, and Jesus comforted her with a message that has become a promise of hope for a multitude of believers who have lost loved ones: "I am the resurrection and the life. The one who believes in Me, even if he dies, will live" (v. 25). But when He went into Bethany, Jesus found a sister who wanted something more.

In Luke 10 Martha was very busy while Jesus taught—straightening, cooking, cleaning, and preparing. It's no wonder she was ready to get out of the house and meet Jesus; she was a doer by nature. But Mary was different. She spent the day sitting at Jesus' feet as he taught. She listened. She considered. She reflected.

Over the week of her brother's death, Mary had plenty to think about. Her internal dialogue might have gone something like this: *I know Jesus has a reason. I know He loves us. But I also know He could have healed my brother. What could be so important to keep Jesus from being here?*

What else do you think Mary might have thought?

What do you imagine Mary's disposition was like when she spoke to Jesus?

What questions are you asking God in your hardship?

I identified greatly with Mary. I tried to comfort myself with all of the right "church answers," but one night in the hospital I found the burden to be too much. Joshua had been throwing up that night, adding to his constant pain. The morphine didn't seem to help. To make matters worse, the chemotherapy had caused painful sores to form not only in his mouth but also on his bottom. He was hungry, but it hurt too badly to eat. Every time he had a dirty diaper, he squealed in pain. At three in the morning I sat in a rocking chair, stroking his head and quietly trying to calm him down.

Sure, I knew this was all for God's glory, but that did little to help me in that moment. I felt like Mary, who, though she trusted in the purposes of Jesus, nonetheless questioned His methodology. Perhaps it was with a note of accusation that she confronted Jesus: "Lord, if You had been here, my brother would not have died!" (John 11:32).

What are some ways Jesus might have responded to Mary's statement?

How do you feel God has answered your questioning during hardship?

How would you have responded to Mary?

According to the Bible, Jesus was "angry in His spirit and deeply moved" (v. 33). This phrase carries a sense of especially strong anger, even indignation and rage. Why was Jesus angry? Was He angry because of Mary's accusing tone? Angry that she didn't grasp the importance of God's glory? Angry that she had a limited focus on her grief?

I don't think so. I believe instead that His rage was directed at the fact that the world is so broken, so sinful, so far away from faith and the gospel that often the only way to convey the message of hope the cross offers is through the suffering of God's children. Though He understood the greatness of God's glory, I believe Jesus was angry that Mary was hurt and had to suffer.

Then the most amazing thing of all happened. No, it's not that Jesus raised Lazarus from the dead. Rather, it's an action recorded in the shortest verse of Scripture in the Bible: "Jesus wept" (v. 35). Can you imagine that?

Jesus wept.

Jesus made no attempt to justify His actions. He didn't explain the nature of good and evil in the world. And He certainly didn't chide Mary for her grief. Instead, He wept with His sister, even though He knew He would turn this funeral into a party in about five minutes.

How does it make you feel to know that Jesus is angered by the necessity of suffering in your life?

As you have experienced hardship or in your current suffering, how have you sensed Jesus' empathy with your situation? What comfort has He offered?

The same thing that happened with Mary still happens with us. God doesn't promise answers. He doesn't promise complete healing this side of heaven. But He does promise presence. And many times the feel of divine tears falling softly on our faces is what we truly need anyway. In this too Jesus is Immanuel—God with us. Always.

Contemplate the fact that Jesus is always with you in your suffering, even though in your waiting He might seem far away. Thank Him for empathizing with your pain. Press into Him and accept by faith His love for you.

identity

Week 3
Group Experience

Looking Back

1. Share one insight you gained from your study of week 2 in the workbook.

2. Did this week's study cause you to look differently at the well-known story of John 11? How?

3. Was Jesus' weeping personally significant to you? Why?

4. Have you ever had to wait for Jesus to respond to your suffering? What did it feel like? How did it affect your faith? What did you learn through waiting?

5. Have your trials caused you to view yourself differently? How?

6. How have you experienced God's presence in your pain?

Watch DVD session 3

Pain strips us
of our marks of
self-identification.

Walking On

1. How do you introduce yourself to people for the first time? What do you want them to know about you?

2. How do tragedy and pain alter our ability to define ourselves?

3. Has that happened to you? How?

4. Was that ultimately a bad thing? Did it feel like a bad thing at the time?

5. Why might God want to strip us of our marks of identity?

Read week 3 and complete the activities before the next group experience.

Video sessions available for purchase at *www.lifeway.com/faithlimps*

identity

Loss is defined as *detriment, disadvantage, or deprivation from failure to keep, have, or get.*[1] That's a fine definition as long as what we have lost is a pair of glasses or the TV remote. But that definition doesn't convey the emotion that comes when we lose something that holds a great deal of personal significance.

Compare, say, the loss of the remote with the loss of a wedding picture. The loss of the first might produce frustration; the loss of the second produces grief over something that can never be recovered.

The greater the personal value of what is lost, the greater the emotional fall that results. That's what I felt as Joshua's chemotherapy continued. I looked back at the way life used to be and realized I had been very comfortable with the way I had defined myself in those days.

After Joshua got sick, though, life radically changed. I needed better insurance benefits, but when I went to work for a large company with a group-insurance plan, I felt that I was abandoning my dream of being an author.

Although I was grateful that God provided the job, I mourned the loss of what once was. A big part of that sense of loss was not knowing who I was anymore. The result for me was a crisis of personal identity. But maybe that's not necessarily a bad thing—at least not in the end. Maybe that loss of personal identity is actually a step toward redemption and restoration. Maybe that's how it happened for Job.

Day 1
Two Choices

The Bible is, among other things, a very honest book. It's full of people who faced death, misery, and hardship, and more times than not, the people in those stories came to the Lord to express their disappointment or confusion about their circumstances. You can't read many psalms or verses in Lamentations without sensing anger; sadness; confusion; and yes, joy emanating from the authors.

Alongside Psalms and Lamentations, though, another book in Scripture exudes this kind of honesty: the Book of Job.

What word comes to mind when you think of the Book of Job? Why?

Can you think of a specific time when you strongly related to this book? What emotions were you feeling at that time?

Read Job 1:1-5. Based on these verses, what kind of man was Job?

Job was a God-fearing man and an upstanding citizen of his community. He had a large family and great wealth, yet he never took any of it for granted. He was continually on his knees before God, even going so far as regularly offering sacrifices on behalf of his children, just in case they had sinned. This was the regular pattern of life for Job, but unknown to him, a cosmic conversation was going on, with Job at the center.

Read Job 1:6-12. What was the essence of Satan's claim about Job's devotion to God?

Read the following verses. Beside each, record what Job lost.

Job 1:13-15

Job 1:16

Job 1:17

Job 2:7

List some things you have lost through a time of illness or other hardship, maybe through a trial you're experiencing now.

By God's permission Satan systematically took apart Job's life, starting with his children. Then his property. Then his physical health. Job was eventually left poor and sick in emotional, physical, and spiritual pain. But why?

If you've read the Book of Job before, you know it was because of a kind of bet—a cosmic wager, of sorts. But Job didn't have the luxury of reading about his story on the pages of a book. He was living the awful reality. And so was his wife.

Read Job 1:20-22. How would you characterize Job's response to his losses?

Read Job 2:9. How was Job's wife's response different from his?

Which more closely matched your response when you experienced great loss in your life?

☐ Job's response
☐ Job's wife's response

At first glance we would be quick to chide Job's wife for her lack of faith and to applaud Job. Scripture clearly says, "Throughout all this Job did not sin or blame God for anything" (Job 1:22). His wife, on the other hand, was ready to cash it all in, including her life.

But here's the thing. Just because Job didn't curse God and die in the beginning chapters doesn't mean he didn't have any questions about his predicament. In this tendency we see a difference between Job and most people who experience loss. Most of the time we medicate ourselves instead of wrestling with the meaning of our circumstances.

Do we turn to alcohol because it tastes good? Do we cheat on our spouses purely from lust? Do we become addicted, entrapped, and unfocused purely from desire? Or are we just trying to escape the reality of our circumstances for a few moments?

Some forms of escape might be more innocuous than others. We might choose entertainment, friends, work, sports, or even church activities instead of a bottle, but in the end we're still running.

What about you? What is your favorite form of medication that dulls your sense of loss?

Why might seemingly harmless activities become harmful when used in this way?

Do you find yourself depending more on these things during a time of suffering? Why or why not?

In fact, we are masters at medicating our pain. When Joshua was sick, I found myself watching more movies and television than I ever had, seeking to escape into a world of fantasy so that I wouldn't have to face another lonely night of questions with God.

The problem with any kind of medication is that it can't permanently take away grief and sadness. It doesn't alter reality. Instead, it keeps us from having to ask the difficult *what, if,* and *why* questions of our lives.

> *The problem with any kind of medication is that it can't permanently take away grief and sadness.*

If the common denominator of life is pain, then a valid question we must ask is what to do with that pain. In the end there are two choices: either we try in vain to escape, or we press hard into the mysteries of the person of God. Job chose the latter.

As you pray today, consider whether you're medicating any pain in your life. If so, what are you using? And why are you doing so? Process these thoughts with God, asking Him to bring to the surface any ways you're depending on something besides Him to deal with your pain.

Day 2
Don't Settle

Medicate or press in. Anyone who has heard the diagnosis, gotten the call from the police, been served the papers, or simply observed the devastation around the world can identify with that kind of choice. Medicating pain, doubt, and questions is certainly a more comfortable way to cope, though it holds no lasting value. No one ever experienced real healing from simply medicating the pain.

No, we must walk the pathway to real, lasting healing and redemption by pressing into the pain and difficulty. But doing that is equivalent to picking at a scabbed-over wound or pressing on an already bruised heart.

> Do you agree that true healing can be found only by walking through the difficulty? Why or why not?

> Is it therapeutic or counterproductive to revisit painful memories associated with a past hardship? Why?

> How did Job choose to press into his pain rather than medicate it?

Pressing in would be much easier if we believed the universe was essentially a cosmic accident, that we're all just bundles of atoms and molecules that happened to come together in the right way. If that's the case, all the trouble and hardship in the world are simply a matter of chance. We were unlucky, and that's why the bad thing happened. Case closed.

But we don't believe that. So if we leave God in the equation, the way we engage our pain becomes problematic because it calls into question everything we think we believe to be true about Him.

> Read Job 1:20-21; 2:10. Why do you think the Bible explicitly points out that Job did not sin in what he said?

> Who, in Job's thinking, was behind his suffering?

> What might be some of the implications for our faith if we came to the same conclusion?

In these verses we see something very curious and very important if we really want to press deeply into the difficulty and aftermath of painful circumstances. We know from the context of the first two chapters that Satan afflicted Job. And yet in these verses Job clearly said, "The LORD gives, and the LORD takes away" (1:21) and "Should we accept only good from God and not adversity?" (2:10).

When Job wanted to press into rather than deny his circumstances, he turned his attention to God. If God hadn't been OK with the spotlight being shined on Him, these explicit statements wouldn't be included in Scripture stating that Job did not sin when he questioned God. We can only conclude, then, that when we suffer, our struggle is ultimately with God.

When we suffer, our struggle is ultimately with God.

When we experience suffering, whom are we more apt to hold responsible—Satan or to God? Why?

Why do we find it difficult to confront God with our questions about suffering?

In what ways have you approached God in times of suffering?

☐ Asked questions   ☐ Assigned blame   ☐ Expressed anger
☐ Expressed trust   ☐ Cried   ☐ Submitted to Him
☐ Other:

It's easier in moments of pain to direct our sorrow, disappointment, and anger at Satan, a broken world, or random occurrence. It's easier to let the blame lie there, but if we do, we rob God of His power and control, and we cheat ourselves out of fully processing the magnitude of who He is. Some argue that God causes hardship. Others say He simply allows tragedies to occur. Pragmatically, though, the result is the same: we suffer, and whether God acts or doesn't act, He is still at the bottom of it. That means our true conflict is with God.

Check the statement that best describes your response to this point.

☐ I feel uncomfortable acknowledging that God is behind my suffering.
☐ I am able to praise and trust God even though He allowed my suffering.
☐ God is in control of everything, my painful situation included.
☐ I would rather blame Satan and leave God out of it.

If we really want to start down the road of asking why we suffer, let's not sell ourselves short of following it all the way to the end. At the end there's God. He's the One in control. He's the only Being in the universe who is sovereign. He is the beginning and the end of all things, including our laments.

That's probably why we're reluctant to follow the trail all the way to the end: if God is at the end, we aren't just asking *why* about our circumstances. We're questioning the foundations of what we think—what we hope—is true. We're asking about the nature of good and evil. We're wondering about the validity of God's love. We're pondering the extent of His compassion and wisdom.

Those are very scary questions to ask, because they shake the very foundations of our existence.

As you pray today, hold in balance the love and the sovereign power of God. Confess your inadequacy to understand, but ask for humility as you move deeper into these mysteries. Feel free to ask Him the question you wrote down.

Day 3
No Easy Answers

No one could accuse Job of stopping short in his quest for understanding. Job fully engaged what was happening to him, insistently asking the hard questions of how and why about the tragedy that had become his life. But not everyone around him was content to do the same.

> Read Job 2:11-13. How would you characterize the initial reaction of Job's friends?

> Why do you think they didn't say anything to him for seven days?

> What value is there in this kind of response?

> Name someone who was present with you during a crisis. What did they do that meant a lot to you?

Seven days is a long time to sit with someone, especially in silence. A long time but a powerful one. On their arrival these three friends did the perfect thing in this situation: they kept their mouths shut and sat with Job. They practiced the ministry of presence, simply being near and hurting alongside their friend.

In fact, this was the foundation of the Jewish mourning ritual called *sitting shiva*. Still practiced today, this ritual revolves around a seven-day period of presence and relative silence. Perhaps this detail is included in the Bible as a subtle reminder that people of faith have a great propensity to say stupid things in times of grief and loss:

- ☐ "She's in a better place."
- ☐ "You'll see him in heaven again someday."
- ☐ "God works all things together for good."

What are some unhelpful things people have said when you were going through a painful time?

We became very familiar with all of these platitudes during Joshua's treatment. Though they are all true, none of them helped very much. In fact, I recall the most help coming one evening when all of our friends came to the hospital during the World Series. We ate cold hotdogs and watched the opening game on a tiny television fixed to the upper corner of a wall. We didn't talk about cancer. We didn't talk about much of anything. But we were there together.

Indeed, it seems that Job's friends better served him when they simply sat and mourned. These men got in trouble only when they started opening their mouths.

Read the first portion of the friends' speeches in Job 4:1-11. What was the explanation Eliphaz offered for Job's suffering?

Read Job 6:14-30. What did Job compare his friends to?

A *wadi* (v. 15) is an ancient Arabian term for an intermittent desert stream similar to a gully or a wash. Job said his friends were like these streams, their loyalty disappearing as quickly as water in the desert. As you continue to read through the speeches of Eliphaz, Bildad, and Zophar, you see that they were bent on finding a logical solution to Job's suffering.

They wanted to figure out the hows and whys too, but they were unyielding in their black-and-white approach. According to them, what happened simply had to be Job's fault, the result of a latent sin in Job's life. To their credit, they were unwilling to call into question God's perfect justice, reasoning that Job needed to own up to his sin.

Job, on the other hand, was equally insistent that he was not to blame. He didn't have a good answer for his severe suffering, but he knew it wasn't as simple as punishment for a sin he had committed.

Is this an arrogant claim by Job? Why or why not?

Read the way Job concluded his argument in Job 31:25-40.

Although Job had lost much, he was still confident of a few things. He knew he had not caused his suffering. And he knew God ultimately had the answers. He refused to conclude anything else.

Check any approaches you have taken in wrestling with the cause of your suffering.

☐ Assumed it was punishment for your sin
☐ Asked God why He allowed or caused this hardship
☐ Rested in knowing God is sovereign
☐ Told God you didn't deserve to suffer
☐ Submitted to your circumstance and asked God to teach you through it
☐ Other:

Ironically, in their attempts to protect God from Job's questions, the friends were actually trying to force Job to settle for something less than the end of his questions. They were pushing him toward logic and reason, and though both have their place, in cases like this what we need isn't either one. When a person hits rock bottom, what they need more than anything else is God.

When a person hits rock bottom, what they need more than anything else is God.

In the very pit of despair, when everything you hold dear has been stripped away to the point that you no longer know who you are, there is a prime opportunity for God to step into the equation. Or rather to reassert His presence, because He's actually been there all along.

Think today about a person in your life who is in pain. Are you practicing the ministry of presence, or are you trying to provide explanations? It might be time for you to pay a visit to sit with them in silence.

Not Why but Who

Job 31:40 succinctly puts the end of Job's search like this: "The words of Job are concluded." What else was left to say? Job had violently clung to the notion that he wanted an explanation from God despite his professed friends' accusations that his suffering was caused by his own sin.

Job had the courage and perseverance to keep on asking, to keep insisting, to keep pressing into the depths of his despair. He refused to stop short on his search, and that search led him into the throne room of heaven. Then something amazing—and perhaps terrifying—happened: God started talking back.

Read Job 38:1-11. What emotion do you imagine God's voice conveyed?

What was the basic message of God's answer to Job?

God answered Job from a whirlwind, a manifestation of God's power. Though Job may have been upright, he was questioning the wisdom and appropriateness of God's choices. It all added up to a simple question that for the life of him, Job couldn't answer on his own: "Why?"

Over the next four chapters God pointed to every imaginable element of His creation, describing His power as He directs everything from the swimming patterns of giant fish to the fall of rain. But here's the troubling thing: nowhere in this diatribe did God ever give Job the answer to his question.

Why do you think God never answered Job's question of *why?*

When you have suffered, have you ever received an answer
to your question of why?

After 37 chapters of accusations, questions, and pain, the answer God gave was
not the *why* Job was looking for. The answer God gave was *who.*

God never cracked the door of eternity and said, "See, this whole thing started
when Satan came walking in here. ... " He never took Job into the future to show
him the good that would come from his struggle. He never revealed the way He
would redeem Job's pain. He never showed Job one of the billions of Bibles that
would be printed in the future, all of which would contain his story. Not one single
answer to Job's specific questions. Just descriptions of Himself.

It seems God doesn't offer answers or promise a glimpse of the inside story. But
although that may seem unsatisfying to us, we've got to ask ourselves the question,
Would knowing why really help?

Do you honestly think knowing all of the reasons for your pain
would help? Why or why not?

I had always thought the question of *why* would be very important to me when tragedy and suffering struck. Surprisingly, though, I didn't care much about the *why* behind Joshua's cancer. *Why* doesn't bring back the lost time. *Why* doesn't gather up the tears we've shed. *Why* doesn't make the ache go away. *Why* doesn't help with the anxiety of the future. But *who* does.

God is the Redeemer of moments both small and large. God gathers our tears (see Ps. 56:8) and holds them in His hands. God is the healer of the soul and the caretaker of the future. *Who* helps tremendously in ways *why* never could.

The truth is, what people in pain need, more than answers, is God. When we are willing to push deep into pain and the questions that come with it, we don't necessarily find all of the answers. But we find God. He is at the core of our questions. And He Himself is the answer to our pain.

> Read Job 42:1-6. What did Job learn from God's revelation of Himself?

> How would a greater understanding of God's power and character help you in your suffering?

How has God shown you more about Himself in a past or present experience of suffering?

Job thought he needed answers; what he got instead was God. The same thing will be true of us. If our quest has God at the root, then God is what we can expect to find. When we do, we can emerge from the dark night of the soul with greater confidence in and understanding of who God is.

> If our quest has God at the root,
> then God is what we can expect to find.

But there's something else we come out with too. When we understand to a greater extent the identity of God, we also come to a greater understanding of who we are in relationship to Him.

Read God's response to Job in chapters 38–41. Praise God for His greatness. Ask Him to show you more of Himself as you pursue Him in your pain.

Day 5
Who He Is and Who I Am

We often think about the grieving process exclusively in terms of people. You lose someone close to you, and you lament that loss in very personal and profound ways. But the same process happens in other areas of life too. Like the moment you realize you're never going to be a doctor. Or when you first learn you can't have children naturally. Or when you realize you may never meet the right person and get married.

You grieve over what your life was supposed to be like as you try and adjust to how your life is. And there is a great sense of loss and sorrow.

What loss have you grieved over in the past or are you currently grieving over?

How has that loss affected the way you view yourself?

How has it affected the way you view God?

These intensely personal losses do more than make us sad; they make us poor.

Think back to the story of Job. How do you think his suffering affected him in the following ways?

Family:
Finances:
Health:
Reputation:

These different components of life essentially form the foundation for the ways most of us identify ourselves. Think about it. When you meet new people, what are the questions you typically ask them after you inquire about their names? You ask about their jobs. Their hobbies. Their families. As the people reveal these details, you form a mental picture of who they are. And the people giving this information think of themselves in these ways as well.

Our families, our jobs, and our reputation are our marks of self-identification. But pain has a way of stripping us of those marks. Tragedy takes away family, friends, finances, health—marks of our identity. In short, pain leaves us in a personal identity crisis.

Pain leaves us in a personal identity crisis.

Thanks to cancer, I found myself with an altered family life, a new career, and crumbling finances. Previously, these were all ways I comfortably identified myself—but no longer. I didn't enjoy meeting people for the first time anymore because I couldn't figure out how to introduce myself. It was as if the things that made me *me* had been ripped away, and in their place was a void.

Have you ever suffered so long or so intensely that you felt more defined by your pain than by who you used to be?

What aspects of your identity has past or present suffering stripped you of?

Describe what it felt or feels like to be in this state.

Poor is a good word for this state of intense emotional and physical pain. You feel impoverished in your sense of self, for you don't have anything left. It's surprising, then, when we turn to the New Testament and read Jesus' words in Matthew 5:3: "The poor in spirit are blessed, for the kingdom of heaven is theirs."

How could Jesus possibly say this kind of poverty is a mark of blessing? Why might being poor in Spirit be a blessed state?

Like Job, we find ourselves in situations in which we have been stripped of all marks of self-identity. And like Job, in our poverty we might trace our questions and doubts to God. Then we'e poised to find a fresh, powerful revelation of just who God is. Poverty teaches us that all we have left is God. But in poverty we're blessed to see that God is really all we need.

It's in seeing God anew that we can also begin to see the blessedness of our poverty. For once we see God as He is, we're ready to be redefined as people. But this time we won't be defined by money or power or prestige or occupation or even earthly family, for all of those marks have been stripped away. We will instead be defined by something better and more lasting.

How do you think God defines you?

The question of identity can be answered only in a moment of crisis, only when something deeply attached to our sense of self is taken out of our control. When we find ourselves in such a state of poverty, the door has been opened for Jesus to say, "Let Me tell you who you really are."

So who are we? We are the children of God. This might sound simple and trite, but the apostle John saw it as a source of great joy: "Look at how great a love the Father has given us that we should be called God's children. And we are!" (1 John 3:1). That truth is incredibly powerful, especially when everything else has been taken away.

> **Describe what it means for you to be a child of God, especially as you face hard times.**

Most of us live our entire lives without even beginning to grasp the immensity of what God has done for us in Christ. We pile job titles, degrees, and accolades on ourselves, and even we as Christians begin to define ourselves by those things. But suffering narrows the cast of characters down to us and God. When all of those other things are gone, we can begin to see our self-worth and identity defined by our relationship to God in Christ.

And that's something that will never change. Pain and loss might strip us of our marks of identity, but no matter what happens, we'll always be children of God.

Pray today as a child of God, poor in spirit but confident in your loving Father. Try to see yourself the way God defines you. Confess your dependence on other marks of identification and repent of them. Place your trust in God to carry you through your pain.

1. *http://dictionary.reference.com/browse/loss.*

Week 4
Group Experience

Looking Back

1. Share one insight you gained from your study of week 3 in the workbook.

2. How do you respond to the idea that God is behind your suffering? How does that view affect your faith?

3. Do you think it would help if you knew the reason for your suffering? Why or why not?

4. Have you ever experienced a loss of identity? What did it feel like? What kinds of questions did it raise?

5. How did you see or are you seeing God rebuild your sense of identity and purpose?

6. How has your experience of pain and struggle been a part of that rebuilding?

Watch DVD session 4

Believing is easier
said than done.

Walking On

1. Which is easier for you to describe—what to believe or how to believe?

2. Why is a time of difficulty an appropriate time to ask not only what to believe but also how to believe?

3. Can you describe a specific instance when it was hard for you to believe?

4. How did you deal with that? What did you learn?

5. Why is it important to believe not only in God's power but also in God Himself?

6. When have you personally experienced that?

7. How do the prayers of people who believe in God sound? What kinds of things do they pray?

Read week 4 and complete the activities before the next group experience.

Video sessions available for purchase at *www.lifeway.com/faithlimps*

faith

How do you believe? It's a tricky question, right? It's not like cooking, riding a bike, or setting up a recording on the DVR, all of which have a step-by-step process. You might argue, "But there are belief classes all over the place! That's what church is!" It's true that those classes teach you *what* to believe about doctrine or biblical history or apologetics. But they don't teach you *how* to believe.

This was a very important question for me when Joshua was going through cancer, because I very much wanted to believe. I wanted to hang on to what I had learned in countless classrooms and small groups about God, His character, and His will. But in the midst of our pain and struggle, I found it increasingly difficult to do so. If only someone would just tell me *how* to believe and not *what* to believe.

Most of us think of believing and loving in the same—although incorrect—category: that both are something you just fall into and out of. One day you love someone or something, only to wake up the next day and discover that you no longer do. When someone asks you how to love, you answer the same way you would if someone asked you how to believe: you just do.

That works great when you feel like loving. Or when you feel like believing. But what about when you don't?

That's when you begin to learn that faith—real faith—takes work.

Faith Is Everything

The writer of Hebrews makes a pretty rock-solid case for the centrality of faith: "Without faith it is impossible to please God, for the one who draws near to Him must believe that He exists and rewards those who seek Him" (11:6).

What does it mean to believe?

Why do you think faith is so important to God?

Do you place the same value on faith that God does?
Why or why not?

Check anything you might value more than faith in your relationship with God.

- ☐ Conduct
- ☐ Service
- ☐ Self-denial
- ☐ Other:

- ☐ Bible study and prayer
- ☐ Biblical values

- ☐ Church attendance

Faith is at the core of everything. It's at the center of our being. It's the driving force behind everything we do.

We fool ourselves when we think belief and trust are related to only some of life's issues. Whether or not a person is a Christian, what they believe is at the core of everything else.

Let's look at a test case of something simple, like eating. That's not about faith, is it? Surely eating is simply a matter of the will; you choose what to eat on a daily basis. But look deeper. Why do you choose cookies over broccoli? Why do you choose soda over water? It's fueled by what you believe. Either you believe junk food will damage your health, or you don't. The firmness of that belief dictates the choice. That's the way it is with everything else too.

> Consider a few other everyday examples. In each of the following areas, how does what you believe drive the choices you make?
>
> Marriage:
>
>
> Parenting:
>
>
> Friendships:
>
>
> Work:
>
>
> Finances:

Especially in the Christian life, every decision we make, whether good or bad, is deeply rooted in belief. When we're tempted to be greedy with our finances, we have to make a choice to believe it's better to give than receive. If we believe that's true, we'll act accordingly. If we don't, we'll keep pursuing money and things. When we're tempted to think our marriages have grown stale and we would be more fulfilled outside them, we have to choose to believe God has placed us together with our spouse. If we don't, we'll quickly find ourselves on a dating Web site posing as someone younger and cooler than our true selves. See how it works?

The list could go on and on and on. At the end of every scenario, once you get past the choices and dig down deeper, you find the question is always one of belief.

How is believing different during times of difficulty?

Why is believing imperative during those times?

If the ultimate question is what you believe, and that belief drives all decisions in life, then painful circumstances are the crucible for faith. To put it another way, suffering reveals what you truly believe. About the way life is supposed to be. About what's important. And about God.

Do you agree that suffering reveals what you truly believe? Why or why not?

What is it about painful circumstances that reveals what you really believe?

How has a present or past hardship tested your faith in God?

Pain is the proving ground for faith. Until you meet opposition in life, as long as things are flowing smoothly and freely, when you have plenty of money, good health, and strong relationships, faith is relatively easy. Not only that, but it's something you don't have to think about much. Your belief system remains theory at that point. That's not to say it isn't real; it might be. But it has yet to be tested in the circumstances of life.

Pain is the proving ground for faith.

But suddenly the diagnosis or the job loss or the grief forces you to look deep inside yourself and wonder, *Do I really believe what I claim to believe, or have I been deluded by easy times in life?*

When you're in the midst of pain, you no longer have the luxury of treating faith as a theory. It must be lived. It must be fought for. At that point faith must be chosen. I fought for faith when Joshua was diagnosed, but the fight wasn't over. Several months into his treatment, his weekly blood test came back with some irregularities. His blood counts were skewed, and the doctor told us that Joshua could be relapsing.

The bile rose in my throat as I thought about starting his treatment over again, possibly this time including a bone-marrow transplant. Suddenly faith was a new kind of hard. It was a new kind of fight. Faith, as we waited for the results of further testing, was work.

As you pray, choose to believe. Spend time confessing God's trustworthiness and your confidence in Him, in spite of your painful circumstances. Ask Him to strengthen your faith.

Day 2
Choosing to Believe

God is very good at doing the same thing over and over again very, very well. Think about a sunrise. It happens every morning, yet it's always beautiful and amazing. Or a thunderstorm. Or children being born. These things fall into the category of what theologians refer to as common graces—God's blessings that fall on the whole earth, righteous and unrighteous alike.

I don't know about you, but I don't have to try very hard to believe the sun is going to come up tomorrow. God is so good and so consistent at these things that we're very rarely conscious that we're trusting Him for them. In some areas, then, we have passive faith—belief that has morphed into assumption.

> Are there areas of your personal life like that? Things you simply expect from God without ever asking for them? Name some.

> Is taking these blessings for granted a good or a bad thing? Why?

When pain invades your life, you no longer have the luxury of passive faith. Suddenly faith is hard. It's something you have to fight for, something you have to choose. Further, you have to choose and fight for faith in the face of evidence suggesting that your faith might be in vain.

My wife and I sat with our bald-headed son eating burritos, waiting for the phone call from the hematologist. She was going to inform us whether the evidence was right, that he had relapsed, or whether something else was happening. I, for one, couldn't seem to get excited about my chicken and tortillas. And I was really struggling to believe.

Read Ephesians 2:8-9. List everything in these verses that is a gift from God.

Was faith on your list? Why or why not?

In our initial salvation experience we're all passive parties who are acted on. According to this verse, we don't conjure up faith; faith is given to us as a gift of God by His grace alone. But after the point of salvation, every Christian is armed with the power of the Holy Spirit. The same power that raised Christ from the dead lives inside us, and the Holy Spirit empowers us to believe. That means, at least for a Christian, faith is a choice, often one that must be made in difficult circumstances.

By its very definition faith is believing something to be real and true even though you can't experience it with your five senses: "Faith is the reality of what is hoped for, the proof of what is not seen" (Heb. 11:1). In other words, if you can see it, you don't need faith. When you can't see—when you're blinded by painful and difficult circumstances—faith is more like work.

Read John 6:22-29. What, according to Jesus, is the work of God?

Why did Jesus equate faith with work?

Somebody in this passage asked Jesus a very simple question: "What can we do to perform the works of God?" (v. 28). We might expect Jesus to have responded with something like "Oh, that's a silly way to ask the question. Faith is the opposite of work. You really don't have to do anything at all; you just believe." Instead, Jesus acknowledged the kernel of truth embedded inside the question: "This is the work of God—that you believe in the One He has sent" (v. 29).

You don't just believe. Not during tough times. Not during pain. During those times believing is hard work.

Believing is hard work.

Has someone ever told you just to believe? How did you respond?

The problem is that many of us are trying hard at the wrong thing. We're trying hard not to sin. We're trying hard to be generous. We're trying hard to read the Bible. But if faith is the driving force behind all of those actions, we should be working hard to believe in each one of those situations.

Think about your own experience of pain or loss. What are you finding it difficult to believe about God and about your situation?

In each of these moments, whatever the circumstances, we must believe in God's resources of grace, power, patience, and hope. We must make the conscious but difficult choice to trust Him, even if we can't see any evidence that He's there.

The point is that we simply can't sit back and wait to feel like believing. If we feel like believing, chances are there's nothing wrong in our lives. When we are hurting, we must work to believe. We must try. But ironically, even our effort at believing must be fueled by what we believe. God is not only the object of our faith but also its source. If we believe He will really supply the power we need, the grace we need, the hope we need, then we can try hard to believe.

Try hard to believe today. As your thoughts drift toward pain and despair, combat them with a conscious effort to trust in the character and wisdom of God. Express your faith in Him.

Day 3
The Hard Work of Faith

There are certain times in life when it's harder to believe than others. That almost goes without saying. But what makes believing doubly difficult during those times is that it's not a one-time choice but one that must be made over and over again. Trusting God is something we must consciously choose many times during the day, especially on those days when we're fighting to hold on to faith.

Read Matthew 6:9-13. What does Jesus' model of praying for daily bread demonstrate about God's character?

What does that request tell us about ourselves?

If we are to pray today for our daily bread, then what must we pray for tomorrow?

Is there a spiritual principle we should recognize in praying for daily bread each day? What is it?

Are you praying each day for faith as you face hardship? Why or why not?

Jesus told us to petition God for our daily bread. That might mean asking the Lord for material provisions today because you don't know where the money or food or shelter is going to come from. But it also might mean asking Him for the strength and grace to simply endure while it feels as if your life is falling apart.

But because we're to ask only daily for our bread, we must wake up tomorrow and ask for tomorrow's bread. The choice to believe and trust must be made over and over again in a myriad of contexts and situations. This is part of what makes the work of faith so hard—that you must persevere in believing in God, day in and day out, and in believing that He will give you what you need.

You must persevere in believing in God, day in and day out, and in believing that He will give you what you need.

Let's return to a question asked earlier in the week and see if your answer has changed: What does it mean to believe?

Standing in our way in the conscious choice and work of faith might be an issue of translation. The English understanding of the word *believe* has its roots in Greek culture and philosophy. The Greeks, a highly intellectual society, thought believing exclusively involved the intellect—that belief is about assenting to a certain set of facts you hold to be true. So the *how* of believing, from that mind-set, involved looking at an empirical set of data and then placing your stamp of approval when you see that it can logically be trusted.

But the Hebrew mind-set is different. In a Hebrew context the word *believe* takes on a different nuance, getting much closer to the idea that believing is hard work.

The Hebrew word for *believe* is used throughout the Old Testament. For example, we find in Genesis 15:6 that "Abram believed the Lord, and He credited it to him as righteousness."

Read the context of this verse in Genesis 15:1-6. What did believing mean to Abram?

Now read Exodus 17:1-12. Can you spot the word *believe* in this passage?

Genesis 15 is pretty straightforward. Abram trusted God at His word. So should we. But the Exodus passage is a little trickier. This passage describes a battle that hinged on a peculiar action of Moses. When Moses, high above the battle in the valley, held his hands in the air, the Israelites won. When he lowered them, the tide turned in favor of the Amelakites: "When Moses' hands grew heavy, they took a stone and put it under him, and he sat down on it. Then Aaron and Hur supported his hands, one on one side and one on the other so that his hands remained steady until the sun went down" (Ex. 17:12). The Hebrew word for *believe* is the same as the words translated into English as *remained steady.*

What do you think believing has to do with remaining steady?

Check the choice that best describes your belief in God during a hardship.

- ☐ Struggling; my faith is failing.
- ☐ Wavering; sometimes my faith falters.
- ☐ Remaining steady; my faith is strong.

Give evidence for your answer.

Believing isn't just about the intellect, as the Greeks thought. It's about action. And perseverance. And sometimes—many times—it's hard work to believe. Sometimes it's as hard as holding your hands above your head for an entire day. It's hard to believe God when the circumstances of life are as heavy as your arms at 3:00 p.m. after you've held them up all day. Yet even in this we believe God will actually help us believe. In a sense we are fighting the battle for belief far below in the valley. And in our story there is someone on the hill with His hands in the air. But the one on our hill, unlike Moses, will not grow tired and weary.

What difference does it make to know that Jesus is continually praying for you as you face hardship?

We know Jesus is even now at the right hand of the Father interceding on our behalf (see Rom. 8:34). He's praying for us as we pray for strength in the battle for faith. His hands never go down.

Thank Jesus today for being your advocate in prayer. Ask Him to help you work hard at believing as you trust that He is interceding for you at the right hand of the Father.

Day 4
The Reality of Hope

Hope, by its very nature, has an element of pain associated with it. That's why we hope at all. If everything were perfect in our present circumstances, then what would we have to hope for? So when you hope, you're implicitly acknowledging that something in your experience isn't as it should be. But when you hope, even on the darkest days, you can always know that because you're a believer, things are going to be OK, even if it doesn't happen until you get to heaven.

But is that the real nature of hope? Is hope simply the feeling deep inside you that things are going to get better?

Is that how you would define *hope?* Why or why not?

Why, in your experience, is hope imperative when life is hard?

What are you hoping for in your current hardship?

If hope is just believing things will get better in heaven if not before, then living in hope can easily turn into a starry-eyed gaze on imagined future events, when things are set right and as they should be. The problem, though, is that you go to heaven only when you die.

That's a difficult truth because it means there are many things we're hoping for that we'll never see this side of heaven. Or to put it another way, as long as we're on earth, some things aren't going to get better. In fact, many things will get worse. Our bodies, our health, the level of morality in the world—these things aren't trending in a positive direction.

If heaven is the basis of your hope, what are the implications for the way you live in the present?

Do you believe it's possible to have real hope not only in the present but also for the present? What is the difference between hope like that and hope exclusively in heaven?

When you find yourself in the midst of despair, heaven feels like a very long time to wait. And the truth is, it might indeed be a very long time to wait.

Read Jeremiah 29:11. Have you ever read this verse before? Do you remember when or why you read it?

Is this verse encouraging to you? Why or why not?

Have you ever read the context of verse 11? Refresh your memory by reading Jeremiah 29:8-14. How long did the Lord say the exile of His people would last?

God's people had been sent into exile. The temple and the great city of God were destroyed. They were captives of evil oppressors living in a foreign land, and then they received this letter from the prophet Jeremiah.

We might be tempted to read Jeremiah 29:11 as if God were saying, "Hang in there. It's almost over. This time of difficulty isn't going to last very long. I'm about to return everything you've lost, and pretty soon you'll be back to normal." But that's not what He said. God refused to give a pie-in-the-sky version of hope that denied the pain of the present.

Jeremiah actually says something like this: "It's going to be 70 years of hurting and pain and exile. It's going to be so long that I advise you to get used to it. Settle down and make a life in the middle of these difficult circumstances. In fact, maybe you should build a house, because you're going to be there for a while."

What is the longest period of time you have suffered from one event or circumstance?

How did you maintain hope through this situation?

What hope does God offer for prolonged seasons of pain?

The good and hopeful news for anyone in pain can't be that it's almost over or we just need to hang in there a little longer. God doesn't urge us to place our hope in a change of circumstances. In fact, in this passage He said just the opposite. He told the Israelites to build houses, plant fields, celebrate marriage, and live their lives.

We can't hope in a change of circumstances; we must hope in something bigger. God calls us not to escape from our circumstances but to embrace His presence and His will in the midst of them. The question of hope, then, is not how we can get out of this situation. The question is how we can embrace God's purposes and God's work in the midst of this situation.

We can't hope in a change of circumstances; we must hope in something bigger.

How do you see God working in your current hardship?

How does the knowledge of God's presence and work in your current situation change the way you view hope?

Pray today that God will open your eyes to see the ways He is working in you and through you in the midst of your pain. Embrace His work in your life.

Day 5
Believing Together

During times of pain we have a tendency toward isolation. We tend to sequester ourselves, justifying our isolation by claiming no one understands what we're going through. True enough. But we also turn inward because of misshapen ideas of strength and resolve. Most of us grew up in North America reading history books and watching movies about self-made men and women. These were the forgers of culture and society, individuals who had enough intestinal fortitude to accomplish great things alone. They were the leaders of the pack, whether in sports, technology, or government. And when the odds were stacked against them, they somehow found the strength inside to keep going. Alone.

Do you have the tendency to turn inward and remain isolated during times of difficulty? Why or why not?

What is the danger of suffering in isolation?

In our culture the true mark of strength is individual achievement. That same idea has heavily influenced North American evangelical Christianity. Alongside those epic tales of individual strength, we hear people in church talk about our personal relationships with Jesus Christ. In our minds, then, the true test of strength in life, spiritual or otherwise, is our ability to take issues on our own shoulders and deal with them.

How does this model contradict the biblical idea of a community of believers? Can you think of specific Scriptures to support your answer?

Read Galatians 6:2. Why would this verse be important during times of difficulty?

God never intended for us to live life alone. In fact, our relational capacity flows from the core of the Trinity itself. God existed from eternity past in perfect relationship with Himself—Father, Son, and Spirit. He created us in His image as relational beings. How, then, can we possibly lift the heavy burdens of life by ourselves?

That's precisely what Paul said in Galatians 6:2. In that book you actually find two Greek words that are both translated *burden*. One of the words denotes a small knapsack that is light and portable, something a soldier might wear to be mobile. The other word, the one used in this verse, is very different. The etymology of the word *burden* in verse 2 implies a heavy weight or stone that someone has to carry for a long time. It refers to something so ridiculously large and cumbersome that it is absurd to think someone could carry it alone. So Paul instructed us to help one another carry the burden.

What in your life matches that description of a burden?

Are you letting others help you carry the load? What is keeping you from allowing others to help?

Specifically in this passage the word *burden* is referring to sin, but Paul knew the issue was deeper than that. In fact, he went on to say that when we carry one another's burdens, we actually fulfill the law of Christ, which demands that we truly love one another.

Unfortunately, pride sometimes keeps those heavy burdens firmly strapped to our shoulders. Sure, we might be willing to help others carry their burdens, but we don't want to trouble anyone else with ours. Consequently, we never unload. We don't talk about our deep feelings of grief and hurt. And we don't acknowledge our disappointment, anger, and bitterness. We just keep right on lifting.

When we choose to take the load exclusively on ourselves, we neglect a great gift God has given to us—the body of Christ. When we find ourselves in the midst of hardship and difficulty, it's easy to forget the promises and character of God. We forget His love. His compassion. His care. His hope and joy. But part of lifting one another's burdens is that we remind one another of the important things we so easily forget.

> Part of lifting one another's burdens is that we remind one another of the important things we so easily forget.

Name someone who has ministered to you in hard times. What quality of God did they remind you of?

Identify a burden you would like a fellow believer to help you with.

Now identify someone who is carrying a burden you could help lift.

We leaned on one another and our friends as we waited for the phone call from the doctor. We allowed our friends to believe with us (or maybe on our behalf). And then we heard the news that Joshua had not relapsed. Something else had caused his blood counts to be abnormal. A great cry of celebration went up, not just from us but also from those who carried the burden with us.

That's how it's supposed to be. We rejoiced together, for we had believed together.

Are you lifting your own burden alone? Who in your life do you need to share the load with? Ask the Lord that question in prayer; then respond immediately. Pick up the phone and get in contact with a burden bearer.

redemption

Week 5
Group Experience

Looking Back

1. Share one insight you gained from your study of week 4 in the workbook.

2. In John 6:29 why did Jesus describe believing as work?

3. Why is believing during hardship more difficult than at other times?

4. What can you share with your group that has helped you learn how to believe?

5. How has God used your suffering to build your faith?

Watch DVD session 5

Redemption means to
buy back. It doesn't
mean to get back.

Walking On

1. Share one way God has redeemed a disappointment from your past.

2. Is it surprising to you to see God at work in disappointment? Why or why not?

3. What would it mean for you to be a steward of your own story of difficulty?

4. How would you have to change the way you look at pain in your life in order to be a steward of that experience?

5. Is that the fullness of what redemption means? If not, what else does it mean?

Read week 5 and complete the activities before the next group experience.

Video sessions available for purchase at *www.lifeway.com/faithlimps*

redemption

Redemption is a multifaceted concept. *To redeem* literally means *to buy back*. For the ancient Greeks the word referred to a large price a slave might save to purchase his freedom. For Jewish readers the word rang with images from the Old Testament. In that context *redeem* not only described the price paid to free a slave but also represented God's great acts in the past. Today the word *redemption* is usually used in conjunction with a coupon. It's something we trade in for something else.

For someone in pain, though, a great promise is associated with the word *redemption*. What is that promise? Does redemption mean you get back everything you've lost? Does it mean at the end, after you've finally begun to move past your grief and mourning, you stand up and boldly declare, "It was all worth it"? We might like to think so. Such a promise might fuel our perseverance during the roughest days, but that's an unrealistic view of what redemption really is.

As our son Joshua entered a pattern of treatment, started prekindergarten classes, and even began to play baseball, life settled into a normal pattern for us. During that time of restored normalcy, I had the luxury to look both forward and backward. I began to take stock of just how much we had lost, and I also began to realize we were never going to get those things back. Redemption, then, isn't a sort of repayment from God. That view falls short of everything our redeeming God wants to do in and through our pain and loss.

Day 1
You Can't Get Back What's Lost

If we want to know something about the true nature of redemption, we would do well to turn to the Old Testament story of Joseph. Here was a man who experienced profound loss in his life. But here was also a man who knew something about God's redemptive hand.

> Do you remember the Old Testament story of Joseph? If not, read Genesis 37:1-11. What kind of person do you think Joseph was as a young man?

> Whom do you resonate most strongly with in this passage—Joseph, his father, or his brothers? Why?

If you begin reading Joseph's story in Genesis 37, you find a petulant and boastful young man. His father favored Joseph above his brothers, and Joseph did little to warrant their affections early in his life. He was proud of things like his coat, the mark of his father's favor. He wasn't afraid to let his brothers and father know that he believed someday he would rule over them and they would bow down to him.

As you can imagine, such an attitude didn't go over too well in the family. The brothers' anger and bitterness ran rampant, and they faked Joseph's death to sell him into a life of servitude. Joseph found himself enslaved in a foreign land, having lost everything precious to him. In fact, the rest of Joseph's life seems a bit like a yo-yo, moving up and down between highs and lows.

Scan the remainder of Joseph's story in Genesis 37–41.
What do you think was the lowest point in his life?

What do you think was his highest point?

Name some things Joseph lost that would never be regained.

Name some ways Joseph grew materially through his life.

Name some ways Joseph grew emotionally and spiritually through his experiences.

Through his years in prison, his elevated status, his false accusations, his further years in chains, and eventually his elevation to the highest position in Egypt (other than Pharaoh), Joseph no doubt had plenty of time to think about everything he'd lost and gained.

Joseph came out of this experience on top. If we fast-forward to the end of his life, we witness a remarkable scene in the Egyptian throne room. Joseph had been in charge of the entire empire for quite some time and had plans in place to care for the people during the intense famine of the day. And lo and behold, who should walk into the throne room but his own treacherous brothers—the same ones who had sold him into slavery years earlier. They didn't recognize Joseph; for all they knew, he had died decades ago. They had come to beg for food because of the famine, and now Joseph held their destiny in the palm of his hand.

Read Genesis 45:1-11. What is surprising about Joseph's reaction here?

What does his response indicate that he believed about God?

In light of this account, how do you think Joseph would have defined *redemption?*

When Joseph revealed his identity to his brothers, he also revealed certain things about his beliefs. These beliefs had been forged in the fires of loss and grief, of great disappointment and anger. This was a moment of redemption. The prideful young man was gone, and what remained was a humble leader who recognized God's good purposes in even the worst of times.

What are some things you have lost through suffering that you will never regain?

How have you seen God change you through your suffering?

Redemption isn't a time when we're repaid for our suffering with prosperity or blessings—a time when the good and the bad even out. Neither is redemption a moment for trite reflections on what we have lost, a time when we say, "Boy, it's all been worth it."

Redemption isn't a time when we're repaid for our suffering with prosperity or blessings.

What specifically do you think the story of Joseph reveals about the nature of redemption?

How does the end of Joseph's story compare to the end of Job's story? Do you think these two men of God would have thought about redemption in a similar way?

Redemption is really about both loss and gain. It's about humbly recognizing that God doesn't promise to return everything we've lost; indeed, part of understanding redemption is knowing we will never get back what was lost. Rather, redemption is a sober acknowledgment of God's good work—not to repay but to faithfully rebuild something different in our lives from the shattered pieces.

Acknowledge to God today that redemption doesn't mean getting everything back you've lost. Ask Him to help you accept that, but also ask Him to open your eyes to ways He is redeeming your circumstances and changing you in the process.

Day 2
Putting the Pieces Together

Job and Joseph both had a realistic view of redemption. They understood that redemption isn't so much about getting back everything that's lost; those dreams, aspirations, jobs, and relationships, in most cases, are gone. And the painful truth is, they may not come back.

And even if they do, they rarely come back in the same form. To put it bluntly, life will never again be as it once was. That's not the promise of redemption.

Do you agree with the previous assessment? Why or why not?

Have you ever gotten back something or someone you thought was lost, only to realize everything is now different than it was? Describe what happened.

Gain and loss. That's redemption. But besides Joseph and Job, another biblical character understood this. He was a prophet who knew both the great joy of the coming Messiah and the searing pain of a home in shambles.

What do you remember about the prophet Jeremiah? List any information you recall.

Jeremiah wasn't called the weeping prophet for nothing. God chose him to be His mouthpiece to all of Judah. The problem was, nobody was listening. Time and time again Jeremiah warned his countrymen of God's impending judgment. He tried to tell them God was going to do the unthinkable: rip their country and heritage out from under them, using a pagan people. But when Jeremiah delivered that message, he was put in stocks. He was ridiculed, and his scrolls were burned.

What do you think Jeremiah's general temperament was like?

How do you think he felt when the destruction he prophesied was finally realized?

When we pick up the narrative in Jeremiah 32, Jerusalem was under siege for a second time. Jeremiah was under house arrest, confined in the city by a royal guard. There was a brief break in the action as the besieging army of Babylon withdrew to face an Egyptian force that was marching toward Palestine. During that time Jeremiah's cousin, Hanamel, visited him, and a transaction occurred.

Read Jeremiah 32:8-12. What was the transaction that took place?

Was this a strange thing for Jeremiah to do? Why?

What did Jeremiah demonstrate by his actions?

What do you think people said behind Jeremiah's back when this occurred?

There might not be a worse time to negotiate a real-estate deal than when your city is under siege from a hostile force. The writing was certainly on the wall: the Babylonians were going to outlast the Israelites, who would lose their land and be deported to a strange place. Nevertheless, Jeremiah literally redeemed the land from his cousin (see 32:8).

At one of the darkest moments in the history of God's people, Jeremiah bought some land. And he redeemed that land in the middle of tragedy. There wasn't a moment of great triumph. There certainly wasn't a time when circumstances evened out. But again, that's not how redemption works.

Read Jeremiah 32:15. What did God say He was going to do?

Notice that God wasn't going to give the people a new land. What might that fact add to our understanding of redemption?

The land itself was a symbol of redemption. God didn't give the people a new land; He worked on the land that had been bought. He didn't take them somewhere different; He returned them to the same hills that once lay desolate. From that desolation He brought prosperity.

We often wish God would swoop down and pluck us out of our circumstances. Countless mornings I walked to our cabinet to prepare Joshua's chemotherapy, and not once did I find that God had miraculously removed it. It was still there, next to the chocolate sauce that covered the bitter taste.

> **When you pray or think about God's redeeming your hardship, which phrase best summarizes your expectations?**
>
> ☐ Delivering me from my suffering
> ☐ Using my suffering to create something new
> ☐ Making things the way they used to be

Let's be clear. Just because our circumstances don't change doesn't mean God doesn't rescue. He rescues us from sin and death and hopelessness. But His rescue incorporates the sad, tragic, devastating circumstances we want Him to remove. Redemption isn't removal; rather, God takes the shattered blocks of our lives and slowly, methodically, but faithfully puts them back together.

Just because our circumstances don't change doesn't mean God doesn't rescue.

In the end there is something new and different, but it's made up of those same pieces of life that once looked so broken on the ground.

As best you can, tell God today that you believe He is redeeming your pain. Acknowledge the slow process, but actively choose to believe in His deliberate work in your circumstances.

Day 3
The Long Way

In a moment we may suddenly understand the fullness of redemption. But the actual process takes much longer. For example, Joseph's life went up and down for decades, and Jeremiah prophesied for years. Today a person might job hunt for months and months and never find anything. Couples can try and try to conceive a child without success. Godly men and women might wait to meet their future spouse for years but never date a promising candidate.

So why doesn't God deliver?

> **Have you questioned God's timing while you were waiting to be delivered from difficulty? Describe the circumstance.**

> **How have you seen God's good purposes come about through long periods of waiting?**

It's tempting for us to look at the amount of time we spend waiting for deliverance, healing, or a change in circumstance and respond with despair. We might even begin to wonder whether God is like a kid with a magnifying glass who burns ants from sadistic pleasure. But there is something greater going on when we are on the long road to redemption.

> **Read Exodus 13:17-19. What significant event had just happened?**

Why does the text state that God led the people on the long road?

Compare your answer to verse 18. What was different between God's perception of the people and their perception of themselves?

The Israelites came marching out of Egypt in battle formation. That's pretty ironic, considering there was not a soldier among them. They were freshly freed slaves; their only experience was in making bricks. And yet they marched out of captivity like a seasoned army.

God, on the other hand, had a more realistic view of the people. Despite the fact that the people considered themselves ready for anything, He knew they would turn back in fear at the first sign of opposition. As if to validate God's knowledge, we find the people, despite the miraculous deliverance they had experienced, quaking in fear only a few verses later at the Red Sea (see Ex. 14:10).

God knew the Israelites better than they knew themselves. The same thing holds true for us.

Can you think of a specific example in your life when you thought you knew what was best for you, only to learn later you did not?

Has God ever kept you from making a decision you thought was the right one, but then you learned it would somehow harm you? Describe what happened.

How do you think God saw your needs differently than you saw them?

We can see a similar principle in Jesus' ministry. Jesus healed and helped a lot of people. Blind people saw, deaf people heard, and dead people lived. But not all of them. Not everyone in the crowds was touched. Not everyone threw away their crutches and unbandaged their wounds. More than a few people walked away from seeing Jesus without a miracle. Why? Did Jesus choose people at random to heal, or was He intentional about not instantaneously healing some?

What might have been Jesus' intention in withholding instantaneous healing in some cases?

Conversely, why did Jesus choose to heal in miraculous and public ways?

It seems most of the time when Jesus healed publicly and immediately, He did so to establish His credentials. These displays of power validated His words and actions. But perhaps there was an equal measure of intentionality in withholding instantaneous healing. Maybe in His wisdom He knew such healing would short-change the ultimate healing He wanted to accomplish. Maybe the same thing is true today.

Think about a time when God withheld instantaneous healing. Identify anything the waiting time revealed about your character that also needed to be healed.

God isn't interested in healing only the physical. He wants complete healing. That's one reason we take the long road. During our four years of daily chemotherapy, we saw God gradually heal not only Joshua's physical illness but also our family as a whole. Through those four years we saw diseases of the heart and soul exposed. Greed. Pride. Self-sufficiency. These all came to the surface.

God isn't interested in healing only the physical.

God knows us better than we know ourselves, and sometimes a prolonged period of dependency and prayer due to painful circumstances serves to bring to light diseases of the soul and character we might not have otherwise seen.

How has suffering taught you greater dependency on God?

How has it changed your prayer life?

Another part of redemption is realizing God is not just interested in changing your circumstances; He's interested in changing you. He wants to completely heal you—body, mind, and soul. As uncomfortable as it might be, sometimes that can best happen on the long road.

Think about your long road of pain and suffering. Confess to God in prayer some of the diseases of the soul that have come to light. Express your desire and confidence in Him to heal these diseases as well.

Day 4
Stewards of Experience

If it's true that God intentionally takes us on the long road because He knows us better than we know ourselves, it must also be true that not a single experience in our lives is ever a waste of time. God is faithful to redeem every situation we're in by using it to fashion us into the people we were meant to be. He rebuilds us from the ground up, using the shattered blocks of our lives as building material.

Read 2 Corinthians 1:3-4. Note the progression in this passage. _____ comforts us. We comfort _____ with _____.

How have you seen this progression in your own life?

One of the clearest ways we see redemption in action is in our relationships with others. God puts us in one another's lives to carry others' burdens and to comfort one another with the comfort we ourselves have received from God. In this way we actually become stewards of our experiences.

What is a steward?

Do you usually think of stewardship in terms of your experiences? Why or why not?

Why might it be appropriate to do so?

How might doing so change your perspective on your life experiences, especially hard times?

Stewards are caretakers; they're those entrusted with a resource in order to responsibly make the most of it. We typically think of stewardship in terms of finances, but stewardship applies to all areas of life. Just as God gives us financial resources, He also gives us talents, families, relationships, and experiences. Even negative ones.

The same expectation applies to our experiences as it does to our money: we're expected to be responsible caretakers of what God has done in and through us. We're to make the most of the story He has given us to live.

If we began to have a more all-encompassing view of stewardship, we would see there's indeed no wasted time, even the time we spend waiting for suffering to end. God is always working, moving, changing, and redeeming. Those actions are played out in our experiences, but they're not given to us just for our own sake. They're given so that we can be conduits of God's compassion, wisdom, and knowledge to others.

Read Genesis 12:1-3. How do you see the principle of stewardship at work in God's directions to Abraham?

Was Abraham blessed for his own sake? What was God's intent in blessing him?

Just as Abraham wasn't to hoard all of God's blessings but pass them on to all nations of the earth, we mustn't hoard what we gain from our painful experiences in life. We must pass on the hard-fought lessons of wisdom, compassion, and redemption to those around us.

We must pass on the hard-fought lessons of wisdom, compassion, and redemption to those around us.

What are some lessons you have learned from suffering that you could share with others?

When we accept that responsibility, we'll begin to become aware of ways God skillfully intertwines our experiences with those around us.

After a painful circumstance, have you ever been surprised to encounter someone going through a similar situation? Did that encounter cause you to view your own experience differently? How?

Did it cause you to view God differently? Why or why not?

If possible, name someone who is going through the same hardship you are. Identify a way you can show compassion to that person.

When you begin to consider just how intricately the hand of God weaves together misfortune and hope, laughter and tears in the lives of all His people, it's truly humbling. God is constantly moving in ways we can't understand and fathom, working for the good of all who love Him (see Rom. 8:28).

That's why we write books. Or share stories. Or empathize with someone in pain. Cancer wasn't the story we would have chosen for ourselves, but it's nevertheless the one God entrusted to us. The question, then, is whether we will steward it well.

By His grace we're trying.

Pray today that God will bring you into contact with someone to whom you can show compassion. Ask Him to help you learn the lessons from hardship that He wants you to share with others.

Day 5
Peace

In His acts of redemption, God puts back together the pieces of our lives. He positions us to be conduits of His compassion to others. When we begin to see these aspects of God's work and character, we begin to experience the true peace that comes with redemption.

> Read Philippians 4:6-7. According to Paul, what leads to peace?

> What kind of peace did Paul describe?

> What do you think it means to have peace that surpasses understanding?

What a radical way to live. This is the kind of life, Paul admitted, that doesn't really make sense. This kind of peace is beyond circumstances. It's bigger than circumstances. And that's why it surpasses understanding: because it's not tied to things getting any better or any different. Yet this is precisely the state we can experience when God redeems our suffering.

But to really grab hold of that kind of peace, we must confront our distorted idea of what peace really is. Take our own example. Four years after Joshua was diagnosed, a hundred or so people gathered together with an enormous cake and one small pill. Joshua had begun to swallow his pills by then, so we didn't need chocolate sauce. With one swig of Coke it was over. The last pill was taken. And we celebrated God's faithfulness and a healthy son.

If you have arrived on the other side of a particular hardship, have you been able to experience peace? Why or why not?

I'll admit that even driving away from that party, I struggled with fear. Where would we go from here? Would Joshua be OK? Would there be side effects in the future? All of these thoughts caused me to wonder about the nature of this peace I was supposed to have.

What is your own definition of *peace*?

We typically think of peace as the absence of conflict. That's certainly not a bad goal to shoot for, whether in politics or life. But that's not a biblical definition. Biblically, peace is bigger than the absence of conflict.

Peace is bigger than the absence of conflict.

The Hebrew word for *peace* is *shalom*. The word is frequently used in the Bible and even still in the vernacular of ethnic Jews today. When you wish someone shalom, you're not just wishing them a lack of conflict. Sure, it would be nice for them to have a life without war, but the literal definition of *shalom* means *completeness*. When you pass that word on to someone, you are saying, "May you have a life that is whole."

What might be the link between peace and wholeness? Why is a life at peace also a life of wholeness?

Does your life feel whole? Why or why not?

Why might peace be a particularly difficult characteristic to have after periods of pain and loss?

Wholeness seems to contradict the very idea of pain. How can you be whole when you're grieving over the loss of something? We can answer that question only by experiencing God's work of redemption. For when you start to see and embrace His redemptive hand, you see that peace doesn't come from any earthly possession. Wholeness isn't a by-product of finances, relationships, health, or career. You can have all of these things and still not be whole.

True peace comes only in grasping what we have been given in the gospel.

Read the following verses. What do they all have in common?

Romans 1:7

1 Corinthians 1:3

2 Corinthians 1:2

Galatians 1:3

Why do you think Paul began so many of his letters with the greeting "Grace and peace"?

The gospel is fundamentally about grace. In His grace, completely devoid of anything we can offer, God has loved us. Passionately. So much that He died for us. That grace leads to peace—to wholeness. Perhaps for Paul these two words embodied that tremendous message of good news.

In the gospel fractured and broken people are given the gift of life through the life of another. In Christ we become complete and whole—people who lack nothing.

Maybe you're experiencing hardship now, or perhaps you've been through suffering but don't enjoy the peace we're talking about. How does reflecting on the miracle of the gospel change your perspective on your pain?

Paul wrote that we have amazing blessings in Jesus Christ: "Praise the God and Father of our Lord Jesus Christ, who has blessed us in Christ with every spiritual blessing in the heavens" (Eph. 1:3). "My God will supply all your needs according to His riches in glory in Christ Jesus" (Phil. 4:19). No matter what happens to us, no matter what we might lose, we'll always be rich in Christ. We lack nothing in Him. We are completely whole.

Consider today that in Christ you are rich. Praise God for every spiritual blessing He has given to you. Rejoice that these blessings will never fade. Take hold of the wholeness that has already been given to you in Jesus.

limp

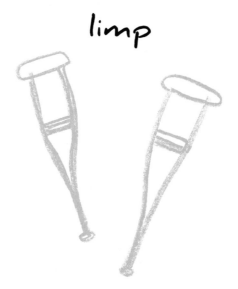

Week 6
Group Experience

Looking Back

1. Share one insight you gained from your study of week 5 in the workbook.

2. Did your understanding of redemption change at all this week? How?

3. Share a brief example of how you have seen God redeem a circumstance of pain or hardship in your life. What did He teach you about His purposes through your experience? About His character? About a walk of faith?

4. This is your last group session, so think back over the entire study. How have you seen your attitude toward pain and difficulty change?

5. Has your prayer life changed? How?

6. Do you feel that you know God better as a result of the experiences you have had and the things you have learned in this study? Do you know yourself better? In what ways?

Watch DVD session 6

Limping isn't a
bad way to walk.

Walking On

1. In what ways have you been marked by your life experiences?

2. Why do you think the Bible uses the word *walk* to describe a believer's relationship with God?

3. How does someone who has dealt with difficulty walk with God differently?

4. How are you walking with God differently as a result of suffering in your life? What forms of self-reliance have you abandoned? How has your identity changed as you have wrestled with God through hardship?

5. State in one sentence what you will take away from your time in this study.

Read week 6 and complete the activities to conclude your study of Faith Limps.

Video sessions available for purchase at *www.lifeway.com/faithlimps*

limp

What will become of those who hurt deeply in this life? Much of the answer to that question depends on what they do with their pain. All of us hurt, but not all of us embrace the pain and the God who can be found in the middle of it. Many of us simply shelve our experiences, working hard not to think about what happened in the past and hoping things can simply go back to normal.

Perhaps life can be normal again, but it won't be the same. No doubt our family's experience with cancer would mark us; our lives would be forever altered. However, the question is what kind of difference we would let it make. Would it be the kind of difference that always seeks to recapture what is lost? Would it be the kind of difference that denies anything has been lost at all? Or would it be the kind of difference that can be found only by engaging the difficult questions of faith in a broken world?

That's the question for anyone who has been marked by pain. What kind of different will we be?

If we engage the role of faith in our suffering, we choose to ask the difficult questions. We choose to confront the pain in our lives. And we choose to wrestle with God through it all. The kind of person who does that will never be the same. They will be marked by their experience, and this mark will go with them throughout their lives.

Day 1
Walk

If you've been around church very long, you've probably heard the phrase "personal relationship with Jesus Christ." It's a fine phrase, for it expresses many biblical ideas. Our relationship with Jesus is indeed personal; God deals with us on a one-by-one basis. And it's a relationship; like any relationship, it includes conflict, arguments, laughter, and tears. It can either be developed or neglected. And it's with Jesus Christ—Jesus, the Messiah, God in the flesh.

The only problem with the phrase is that it's not in the Bible. When the Bible describes how we interact with God, we don't find this term anywhere in its pages. Sure, the ideas are there, but the terminology is absent. Instead, when the Bible talks about the way we relate with God as believers, it frequently uses a single word: *walk.*

> Why do you think the biblical writers used the word *walk* to describe our relationship with God? How is our relationship with God like a walk?

> Read the following verses in several translations, if possible, and identify ways the word *walk* is used.

> Genesis 5:24

> Micah 6:8

> Ephesians 4:1

> Ephesians 5:2,8,15

The prophet Micah said God requires people to humbly walk with Him. Paul frequently used the word *walk* in his letter to the Ephesians to describe the way believers are to live as followers of Christ. Walking was the defining characteristic of the mysterious Enoch, who fellowshipped so closely with God that he didn't experience death. As believers, we are meant to walk with God.

As believers, we are meant to walk with God.

A walk is about moving forward. It's about progressing toward a destination. It's a journey, and what is life if not a journey? For believers life is a journey accompanied by God. We walk together, talk together, laugh together, and cry together, always moving forward as He guides and directs.

Sometimes those steps come easily. During those times our relationship with God feels more like a run than a walk; every moment it seems we experience God's presence in an almost tangible way. We walk with a spring in our step, confident of God's activity, blessing, and direction.

Describe a time in your life when you walked closely with God.

In contrast, characterize your life walk when you have experienced pain. How does suffering change your walk with God?

When painful circumstances dominate the landscape of life, our walk with God feels more like trudging through quicksand. Every step becomes an arduous effort, a conscious choice to put one foot in front of the other.

Fortunately, most experiences like this are temporary. We struggle in our walk for a while, but our steps eventually become easier again. But for those who wrestle deeply with profound questions of life and faith, they find that though the individual steps might become easier, they are nonetheless different. They are marked. As you walk forward with God, you find that your entire spiritual gait has changed.

You might say your walk has become a limp. You continue to move forward with God, but you do so in a much different way.

> Can you relate to the analogy of limping along in life after going through suffering and pain? Why or why not?

> Read Genesis 32. Record the events in this chapter on the following time line.

In Genesis 32 we find a man who knew what it was like to have everything go well in life. We also find a man who knew what it was like to wrestle with God and to be marked by that wrestling as he walked forward.

Jacob knew what it meant to limp.

Ask the Lord for wisdom and insight into Genesis 32 as you continue your study this week. Pray that He will use this passage to reveal truths to you about your walk with Him.

Day 2
Deceiver

Genesis 32 is the climactic moment in the life of Jacob, the son of Isaac, the son of Abraham. This passage chronicles an instance in Jacob's life when he was camped alongside the Jabbok River. The next morning he would go across to meet his long-estranged brother, Esau. Jacob wasn't looking forward to it.

> **What do you remember about the relationship between Jacob and Esau?**

> **Read Genesis 25:24-34; 27:1-10. Based on these passages, how would you characterize Esau?**

> **Now list characteristics of Jacob.**

Let's make no pretense about what had led to this moment. Jacob had always been a shifty, scheming, deceptive man. And he'd been that way a long time.

Jacob was a twin; his brother, Esau, was born mere moments before he was, and Jacob came out grabbing his older brother's heel. That's how he got the name Jacob; the same Hebrew root is found in the verb meaning *to take by the heel.* However, that same root also means *to deceive.* This description turned out to be accurate.

How do you think Jacob viewed the relationships in his life?

Do you think you would have liked to be his friend?
Why or why not?

As the boys grew, Jacob became manipulative and self-serving. As the older brother, Esau was assumed to have the primary blessing of the family: the birthright. And yet Jacob took advantage of Esau's extreme hunger one day and convinced his brother to sell him the birthright for a bowl of lentil stew.

Jacob's deceptive nature surfaced again when his father, Isaac, was dying. When Isaac was about to give his older son, Esau, his blessing, Jacob deceived his father and stole the blessing right out from under him. This was the last straw, making Esau mad enough to kill his brother. So Jacob went to live with his uncle, Laban.

How would you expect Jacob to behave after he was chased from his home?

Read Genesis 30:29-39. How do you see Jacob's nature emerging here again?

Despite having to flee for his life, Jacob had made self-service and deception work to his advantage up to that point. He continued to prosper with Laban. Over the next two decades or so, Jacob deceived his way into gaining a tremendous amount of wealth for himself, even going so far as manipulating the color of newly born goats. So when Jacob finally left Laban, he left as a con man who had fleeced yet another person out of their property. But all that was about to change. In Genesis 32 Jacob had run out of places to go, so he was going back home. But back home was where his robbed, deceived, and angry brother, Esau, was. Jacob was confronted with a crisis.

Put yourself in Jacob's place that night. Given his personality, what might he have done to try and deal with the situation?

Have you ever done something similar, relying on your own cunning or another natural strength to get out of a crisis? If so, describe what you did.

Though an outsider looking at Jacob's life might have observed that Jacob was cunning but unscrupulous, looking out only for himself, something else was happening behind the scenes. The sovereign hand of God was at work in Jacob's life, whether or not Jacob recognized it. God had decided long before Jacob's deception that the blessing given to Abraham would pass through him. God had also decided long before that Jacob would marry Rachel. God had been directing events for years through the major events in Jacob's life like birth order, as well as the seemingly insignificant ones like the number of spots on a goat.

*The sovereign hand of God
was at work in Jacob's life.*

Up to this point God had been content to let Jacob think he was responsible for it all. But no longer. God had been engineering this moment of crisis for a long time. Perhaps the same thing might be true for us.

> Think about a crisis of past or present hardship in your life. Can you look back and see ways God orchestrated events that brought you to a point of crisis in your walk with Him? Describe some ways He might have been at work.

Perhaps God, through our own moment of crisis, might bring us to the Jabbok River as well. But for what purpose? What might we find there?

Imagine yourself praying in a crisis you have faced or are facing. What do you see? What do you sense? Consider how the events in your life have led to this point of confrontation. Where is God in all this?

Day 3
A Divine Opponent

As Christians we claim that we live by faith and trust in God. Practically, though, most of us live with the same philosophy as Jacob: we use self-reliance and manipulation of circumstances to our advantage. We trust in our ability to interview, to network, to form relationships. We trust in our earning potential, our insurance plans, and our trust funds. In short, we trust ourselves. But in a moment of true crisis, we come face-to-face with our own inability and utter powerlessness to bring about any real change in our lives. We're confronted with our own mortality, with the fact that our days are like dust, and we can't do anything about it.

Do you agree that we primarily trust in ourselves until forced to do otherwise? Why or why not?

What natural abilities do you tend to rely on instead of God?

☐ Physical strength
☐ Intellect
☐ Other:

☐ Deception
☐ Business sense
☐ Personality

☐ Common sense

What is so appealing about self-reliance?

Why is such a life displeasing to God?

That's where Jacob was at the river that night, and that's where we find ourselves on diagnosis day. Or pink-slip day. Or the day the papers were served. That's why earlier in Genesis 32 Jacob had sent his family ahead of him. When he came to this moment of crisis, he knew he might very well die because of his past life of deception. He had nothing left. No plan B. No clever tactic. So he started to pray, as we all do in those moments (see v. 9). As the saying goes, there are no atheists in foxholes. Neither are there many atheists on riverbanks, I suppose.

Later, in the stillness of the night, when Jacob was most alone, most threatened, and most out of ideas, a figure stepped out of the shadows. And he was much more imposing than Jacob's brother, Esau.

> Read Genesis 32:21-24. What do you think went through Jacob's mind when he saw the man?

> What was your default reaction when you last faced a moment of crisis?

God waits for us at these moments, times when we have to decide whether to go forward in our natural strength that has gotten us this far or to send up a cry of desperation. God stands there in the shadows of pain, looking through the haze at our quivering forms. And He's there because He wants to wrestle.

> What does it mean to wrestle with God?

> Why do you think God wanted to wrestle Jacob?

Maybe the reason for wrestling is intimacy. You can go only so far in a relationship without wrestling. You might have several casual friendships in which there has never been an argument or a disagreement, but relationships of real depth always involve conflict. It's through conflict that real intimacy is developed.

It's through conflict that real intimacy is developed.

Why should a relationship with God be any different? After all, wrestling by its very nature involves close contact. When you wrestle, you smell someone's sweat. Your head is pressed against their chest. You're locked in close combat.

Jacob knew about God. He must have heard stories about God and His covenant from his grandpa, Abraham, and his father, Isaac.

What stories of faith might have been told in this family?

Why, then, do you think Jacob was a man of self-reliance rather than faith?

Though he might have had some background in what it means to walk in faith, Jacob was a classic avoider of conflict. He was much more prone to manipulation than he was to hashing things out. When the going got tough, Jacob cut and ran. He ran from his dad. He ran from his brother. He ran from his uncle. But God would no longer let him run.

Has God ever forced you to confront conflict after you have continually tried to avoid it? Describe one experience.

Identify a time of suffering in your life that resulted in greater intimacy with God. What role did wrestling with God play in this process?

When we find ourselves in the same situation as Jacob, we have a choice: we can either deny the conflict, or we can engage God in an uncomfortable wrestling match. This is what God wants, for it's by this conflict that He moves us from shallowness to intimacy in our relationship with Him.

What about you? Are you ready to wrestle with the divine?

Consider that question as you pray today. Ask God whether now is your time to wrestle through your lingering issues of trust. Confront your tendency to trust in yourself rather than Him.

Day 4
What Is Your Name?

HELLO

During times of great pain, as we choose to walk deeply into them, we find ourselves locked in a struggle with God. On our end we ask questions about His character, His wisdom, and His plan. But God's goal for the wrestling match is much different.

As in Jacob's case, God is wrestling away our attempts to direct our lives and trust in ourselves. Our faith is what God is after; He wrestles us for our trust. Up to that point Jacob had lived his entire life trusting in his own abilities. He wouldn't give over the control of his life easily, so he wrestled until daybreak.

Read Genesis 32:24-26. Why do you think Jacob was so reluctant to give up?

Is that a good trait or a bad trait in his character? Why?

How might God redeem that kind of stubbornness? How might it be useful and God-honoring when rightly directed?

What characteristic have you stubbornly tried to hold on to even though God has tried to wrestle it out of you? Why do you think this quality is so important to you?

Jacob wouldn't let go. In fact, he even made one last-ditch effort to hold on to control of his life. He held on and brazenly, through gritted teeth, exclaimed, "I will not let You go unless You bless me" (v. 26). Jacob was still determined to assert his self-direction and self-reliance.

Do you really think God could not overcome Jacob?

Why, then, did God allow the wrestling to go on so long?

Describe a wrestling match between you and God.

What was the outcome?

Even in moments of crisis when we know there's nothing we can do to help ourselves, we're still hell-bent on our own self-preservation. Perhaps that's why God let this match go on so long; not only Jacob but we too must be brought to the absolute end of ourselves. Even though we may acknowledge that God's way is best, we nevertheless hold with white knuckles to our own ability to fix things in our lives.

> *Even though we may acknowledge that God's way is best, we nevertheless hold with white knuckles to our own ability to fix things in our lives.*

In the midst of Jacob's hanging on, God did something that changed everything.

For the Hebrews, a name was the essence of the person's identity, and Jacob had lived up to his moniker: he was a deceiver. Can you see the light go out of Jacob's eyes with this question? He was straining with exhaustion, holding on with all his might, when suddenly his entire life came into focus with just one question. With this question God forced Jacob to examine the way he had been living his life. Jacob suddenly had to own up to his true character.

By this point Jacob's arms must have felt weak. Maybe his head drooped. In shame and frustration he felt his resolve leave him, and he had to answer honestly, maybe for the first time in his life, "I am a deceiver."

When we wrestle with God, there's no room for self-deception. There's no room for pretense. We're laid bare before Him, and in His grip we must acknowledge who we really are. Through clinched teeth we hear the truth of who we are. Liar. Addict. Manipulator. Doubter. Deceiver.

What a hopeless situation! We're brought to terms with the truth of ourselves in the midst of that painful embrace, and we don't like what we see. The weight of ourselves threatens to crush us. But then the astonishing thing happens—to us just as it did to Jacob.

Read Genesis 32:28. How did God respond to Jacob's honesty?

As you think about your own wrestling matches with God, in what way is God's response to Jacob significant for you?

The One who named the stars in the sky whispers a new name in our ear.

As you pray today, try to feel the grip of God and hear Him ask you what your name is. Own up to your true character. And then allow the God who loves you to speak a new name to you.

Day 5
Limping Along

A new name. More importantly, a new identity. A new defining mark of who we are. That sounds a lot like the gospel to me. We once were lost, but now we're found. We once were enemies, but now we're children. We once were alienated, but now we have a seat at the table of the King.

God gives us a new name in Christ. It's a new mark of identification. Though that happens when we first receive Jesus, from time to time we need to be reminded of who we are.

> **Read Genesis 32:25-28. What was Jacob's new name?**

> **How does that name reflect both who Jacob was and who he would be in the future?**

Jacob emerged from the struggle with a new understanding of himself. He wasn't the deceiver any longer; he was Israel, *God contends.* Jacob means self-sufficient. Israel is a reminder of human frailty. Jacob means counting on yourself; Israel means trusting in God. Jacob is a commentary on human ability; Israel is an expression of God's power. Jacob went forth from his struggle no longer the self-sufficient self-truster but as one who had placed his faith in God to preserve him. And that name became the name by which the people of God are still known.

> **How might the name Israel, *God contends,* have encouraged the people of God in the future?**

How might that name express the way God wants you
to emerge from your own struggle of pain?

We enter the wrestling match with God so sure of everything, only to find our worlds crumbling within His grip. We are forced to reckon with who we really are, in all our doubt, fear, and selfishness, but God doesn't leave us there. He's not just fighting for the sake of fighting; He's fighting for our trust, and when He has it, He wants to give us a new name too.

Son. Daughter. Treasured possession. Inheritance. Saint. Brother and sister of the King of the universe.

Do any of the names above hold special significance for you?
Which one? Why?

Read Genesis 32:25. What else did Jacob emerge from the
struggle with?

What significance does a limp have for a walk with God?

Jacob left the wrestling match that night with a new name, but that's not all. He was also marked by the struggle with a limp. If our relationship with God is framed in terms of a walk, Jacob limped. As he walked forward with God, his walk was marked by the struggle. Such is the case with all who struggle with God. Coming out of crisis, we all limp. We limp emotionally, spiritually, and sometimes even physically along the journey of life.

Do you have a limp as a result of a struggle with pain and suffering? Describe it below.

Is that limp a good or bad thing? Why?

As Jacob's walk was marked by a limp from then on, the way we walk with God will always remind us of our past struggle. We never really escape our pain; it's always with us. But the limp also reminds us of our own frailty and of God's divine power. This is the essence of trust: an intimate knowledge of our own inability and an acknowledgment of God's power and might.

Comforting, though, is the fact that Jesus knows what it means to wrestle, and He knows what it means to be wounded by the struggle. He certainly wrestled in the garden the night before His death. In that wrestling match Jesus relinquished His trust to God and through drops of blood confessed His faith: "Not My will, but Yours, be done" (Luke 22:42). And afterward He was marked too, except His marks were wounds in His hands and side.

I suppose we would look like a ragtag bunch on the road together—Jesus with His scars and all of us with our canes, all limping together down the road of life. But someday, when we get to the end of the journey and compare wounds from our time on earth, we'll realize that ours were really light and momentary struggles in the light of eternity with God (see 2 Cor. 4:17). We'll celebrate together that God loves us enough to wrestle us for our faith. And our limps and wounds will remind us that in any circumstance He is ultimately, divinely, lovingly, and abidingly able.

Praise God today as the One who contends for you in ways you are not able. Thank Him for any limps reminding you that He is your life and your strength. Express your faith in Him.

faith limps